The Knowledge

Smashin' FASHION

By Michael Cox
Illustrated by Philip Reeve

107878

Hippo

Scholastic Children's Books,
Commonwealth House, 1–19 New Oxford Street,
London WC1A 1NU, UK
A division of Scholastic Ltd
London ~ New York ~ Toronto ~ Sydney ~ Auckland

Published in the UK by Scholastic Ltd, 1998

Text copyright © Michael Cox, 1998
Illustrations copyright © Philip Reeve, 1998

ISBN 0 590 19719 3

All rights reserved
Typeset by TW Typesetting, Midsomer Norton, Avon
Printed by Cox & Wyman Ltd, Reading, Berks

2 4 6 8 10 9 7 5 3 1

Contents

Michael Cox chooses his clothes very, very carefully, and often spends months on end wandering around top fashion stores looking for just the right sort of flared socks to go with the tweed anoraks and squirrel-hair jodhpurs that he is so fond of wearing.

Michael believes he cuts something of dash as he struts his stuff on the local high street, and says he finds the admiring shrieks and hoots of passing shoppers and motorists most flattering.

Philip Reeve always dresses at the height of 90s fashion. But, unfortunately, it's the height of *18*90s fashion. Luckily, when he isn't busy drawing, he spends his time walking on hills, where only sheep get to see his enormous tweed trousers.

INTRODUCTION

Fashion is smashin' fun, isn't it? In fact, can you imagine what life would be like if we all wore the same clothes all the time?

Yep, the world would be a pretty dull place if we didn't have fashion at all. Even wearing a school uniform, nowadays, most of us manage to find small ways to make it daringly different. Our clothes and the way we wear them can say an awful lot about us.

Fashion can do a lot for you too. It can make you look great (or at least *think* you look great) and give you confidence ... or disguise you completely. It can give other people something to admire and enjoy ... or giggle at. And it certainly gets people talking.

But where did it all begin? Some people say it started in Europe in the 14th century, when wealthy people wanted to show everyone else just how well off they were by parading around like peacocks in really expensive clothes.

Others disagree. They reckon fashion became smashin' much, much earlier and that people have been dressing up in amazing outfits and even painting and decorating their bodies for thousands of years.

One thing we know for sure is that fashion is fascinating. It's full of amazing stories and fabulous facts and outrageous ideas. This book will give you a taste of some of the best fashion stories in history, and some top fashion tips from the creators of style. So if you want to find out:

● which smashin' fashion caused a riot in 19th century London
● why medieval fashion fanatics walked upstairs backwards and
● how to become a superstar fashion designer – read on!

HANDSOME HAIR AND WICKED WIGS

What's *your* hair like? Is it straight ... or curly ... or dark ... or fair? Or an exciting mixture of all four? Does it just sort of sprawl sulkily across the top of your head like a moody labrador on a settee ... or is it always alert, attentive and eager to please? Are you happy with your hair? Do you take one look in the mirror and mistake yourself for a mega-famous film star with the sort of hair that ordinary people would die for? Or are you more likely mistaken for Lassie?

The long and short of it is that hair is a great fashion accessory. Ever since the first hairy caveman mistook his best friend's pet sloth for a newfangled chest quiff and rushed off to the local hairdressers' to get his own cut in the same style, people have been doing all sorts of peculiar things with their hair just to stay in fashion. You'd be amazed at the things they used to get up to – for starters take a look at what those crazy ancient Egyptians did with theirs!

Some ancient Egyptian hairstory
It was the fashion for ancient Egyptian men and women to curl their hair by wrapping it around hot

metal rods and coating it with bees' wax. Then they probably spent ages teasing it into shape (with *honey*-combs?). They made a paste from crushed donkeys' teeth to strengthen it, and to stop their hair from falling out plastered it with a concoction made from dates, dogs' paws and asses' hooves! These Egyptians also used a pretty weird hair restorer made with fat from crocodiles, snakes and lions (which turned slap-heads into fat-heads).

Ancient Egyptian barbers used to work in the street. They didn't even have seats for their customers, so when people wanted a haircut they just knelt down at the side of the road while the barber shaved their head. Egyptian hairdressers couldn't afford their own barber-shops – the overheads were too high (ha, ha).

Some ancient Roman hairstories

The Romans weren't too keen on washing their hair because they believed it would disturb the mysterious and all-powerful spirit which looked after the head (or the school secretary, as we call her today). This reluctance may have been started by an ancient Greek historian called Plutarch who told the Romans that they should wash their hair just once a year, on 13 August. This was the birthday of Diana, the Roman goddess of the moon and hunting (… and all-in-one shampoo and conditioner).

Many noble Romans were vain and wanted to stay looking as young as possible. So if they noticed that their hair was beginning to go a bit grey they coloured it with a dye made from walnut shells, chopped leeks, oil, ashes and earthworms. And instead of wearing wigs, some bald Romans actually got artists to paint and draw pictures of hairs onto their shiny bare bonces.

I MEANT HAIRS WITH AN "I", IDIOT!

But if bald Romans didn't like the idea of a hair doodle, or hairy Romans fancied a change of image, they could always buy themselves a wig. The most popular ones were made from the hair of recently captured slaves ... particularly fair-haired ones from northern Europe.

OFFICIAL!
FRESH HAIR IS GOOD FOR YOU!
TIRED OF BEING A BRUNETTE? THEN HELP IS AT HAND! TURN YOURSELF INTO A DIZZY BLONDE IN SECONDS! GET DOWN TO
SHAVE-A-SLAVE
YOU PICK 'EM – WE CLIP 'EM!
STOP PRESS – JUST IN!!!!
A FINE CONSIGNMENT OF BLONDE BOMBSHELLS CAPTURED DURING OUR GREAT LEADER'S RECENT BELGIAN CAMPAIGN
DON'T FORGET – BLONDES REALLY DO HAVE MORE FUN (UNLESS THEY HAPPEN TO COME FROM BELGIUM)

Wealthy, and *extremely* vain, Romans had marble busts of their heads made by artists. But in order to make sure that their stone images remained in fashion the busts had detach-able hairdos which could be replaced with whatever style and colour happened to be top of the toffs at the time. Of course, this tradition has now stopped and the busts are out of date, but perhaps we could give Julius Caesar a bit of a restyle.

COOL!

JULIUS CAESAR

The Gauls, who used to live in what is now France, liked to wear their hair long. When Julius Caesar conquered them in 50 BC he ordered them all to get their hair cut. The Gauls weren't too happy about this – in fact it made many of them really bristle!

Boys and curls

In the 17th century, fashionable European men went to tremendous lengths to have the trendiest hair in town. Long locks were the in thing, and cool dudes of the day wouldn't dream of strutting their stuff on a Saturday night without a mass of curls cascading over their shoulders. The real trend-setters also wore something called a cadenette. What do you think this was?

a) a sort of hairnet

b) a single lock of hair that dangled over one shoulder all on its own

c) a small hat shaped like a tea-cosy.

Answer: b) Cadenettes were invented by a French nobleman called Cadenette (*quelle surprise!*). In a moment of sheer hair-brained recklessness, young Seigneur de Cadenette had let one of his long locks dangle rather cheekily over one shoulder and accidentally sparked off a new fashion trend. The local girls obviously thought the young Frenchman was gorgeous and gave him lots of little presents like ribbons and jewellery. Cadenette cleverly tied these gifts (or favours, as they were known) to his saucy strand and sparked another trend!

13

The fashion quickly spread to other countries. In England it became known as a "love-lock". You didn't even need to have lots of girlfriends to have your love-lock loaded down with gifts. You could just pretend.

Hair wig go ... hair wig go ... hair wig go!

Wigs were big in the 17th century and most nobles eventually took to wearing them. The famous London diarist, Samuel Pepys (1633–1703), complained, "I did try two or three periwigs meaning to wear one and yet I have no stomach for it." Maybe he realized that the wigs were meant for his head, and not his tum, because not long after he wrote this he gave in, had his head shaved and bought himself a wig. After all, wigs did have a lot of advantages over your ordinary hair…

Invasion of the wig snatchers

Wigs were very expensive (especially if they were made from human hair) and gangs of professional wig thieves operated in big towns and cities.

Here's one way that the thieves outwitted unwary wig wearers.

This sort of theft became so common that keen wig wearers always got very nervous when they saw anyone carrying a bread basket. Bakers started to carry their baskets on their arm or at an angle on their backs so that people could see that they weren't hiding a small boy.

Smashin' fact
In order to complement their false hairdos some wig wearers wore false eyebrows too ... made from mouse hair!

OH VERY STYLISH!

Forget big hair ... get "themed" hair!

By the end of the 18th century, rich men and women all over Europe were absolutely obsessed with fashion. As a result their hairdos became *very* imaginative and elaborate. Aristocratic women – particularly friends of the fashion crazy French queen, Marie Antoinette (1755–1793) – believed that the only way to be truly fashionable was to be seen wandering around with a small theme park or a famous scene from history attached to the top of their heads. The women were vain, rich and power-ful, and they had whole armies of servants at their command and oodles of time on their hands, so what better way was there to while away their empty days than trying to out hairdo each other with one of these...

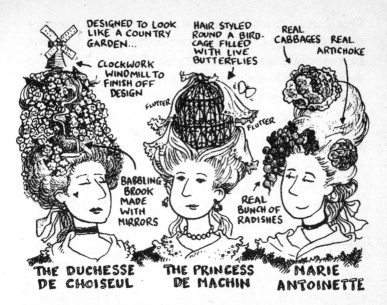

DESIGNED TO LOOK LIKE A COUNTRY GARDEN...

CLOCKWORK WINDMILL TO FINISH OFF DESIGN

HAIR STYLED ROUND A BIRD-CAGE FILLED WITH LIVE BUTTERFLIES

FLUTTER

FLUTTER

REAL CABBAGES REAL ARTICHOKE

BABBLING BROOK MADE WITH MIRRORS

REAL BUNCH OF RADISHES

THE DUCHESSE DE CHOISEUL

THE PRINCESS DE MACHIN

MARIE ANTOINETTE

Coiffeurs who wouldn't let it lie! – *how the styles were created*

1 The French coiffeurs (hairdressers) wrapped hair around wire frames (a bit like the ones that flower arrangers use nowadays) and padded out their creations with little cushions made from horsehair.

2 They smeared the whole hairdo with enormous dollops of stuff called *pomade*. This was the 18th century equivalent of hair gel, except pomade was made from lard. That's the fatty stuff that dribbles out of roast beef and pork. Perfume was added to the lard to disguise its smell (whatever for, roast pork smells lovely, doesn't it?).

3 Hair powder was then sprinkled over the whole creation. This was a sort of "designer dandruff" made from bread flour (which was obviously really useful if you wanted to arrange your hair in a bun!).

Sometimes the powder was coloured pink, blue or yellow so that the wearer could match their hairdo to their clothes (or skin ... or teeth?).

4 The hairdresser would then add the finishing touches – bowls of fruit, basket of flowers ... the kitchen sink – whatever seemed appropriate.

Smashin' facts

1 It's tuft at the top! When the Native Americans of the Pawnee tribe shaved their heads they always left just one lock of hair in the middle as a sporting challenge to their enemies. A sort of *"bet*  *you can't catch hold of this and whip my scalp off before I whip yours off"* dare.

2 Some members of the Muslim faith also leave a lock of hair on their shaved head but this has got nothing to do with scalping. It's there so that their god, Allah, can grasp it and pull them into paradise when they die.

One stop chopping

Those 18th century French women didn't go out to get their hair done – their hairdressers visited them at home. For women, the idea of going out for a hairdo is quite a modern one and women's hairdressing salons have only been around since the early 20th century. Men, on the other hand, have been going to barbers' shops since medieval times ... and not just to get their hair cut!

Grease!

If a man went to a barber late in the 19th century they probably wouldn't have offered him surgery (by then they were leaving that sort of thing to the professionals), but they might have asked him if he'd like some bear grease on his hair. At the time bear grease was thought to work wonders for both men's and women's hair. Here's an extract from an advert that actually appeared in *The Times* newspaper in 1793:

Just killed, an extraordinary fine fat Russian bear, at Ross's Ornamental Hair & Perfume Warehouse – 1s. per ounce, to be seen cut off the animal in the presence of the purchaser.

Smashin' facts

1 In 1698, the Russian emperor, Peter the Great (1672–1725), tried his hand at a bit of amateur barbering. After deciding that he wasn't too keen on beards, he personally cut off the whiskers of all the most important noblemen in Russia. Anyone else who felt like wandering round with a hairy face was made to pay a beard tax. Beard inspectors were stationed at town gates and issued travellers with beard licences made from copper discs – anyone who refused to pay for the licence had their whiskers forcibly removed.

2 In the 17th century ferocious warriors known as the Manchus charged out of Manchuria and knocked seven bells out of their nextdoor neighbours, the Chinese. They established an empire which became known as the Ming Dynasty. The proud new Manchurian conquerors didn't want the Chinese to forget that they'd been defeated by their brave and skilful cavalry (horse soldiers) so they passed a law saying that all Chinese men had to wear their hair in a "pony" tail.

Drastic cuts – 200 years of hairstyles that made the headlines

IN THE WOMEN'S SALON

Oreilles de chien
French for 'dog's ears' – became fashionable in 1789 in France and England.

Ears muffs – 1840s
Centre parting – ropes of plaited hair with artificial 'horse hair' knots over ears.

Chignon – 1860s
False hair pieces – like droopy sausages – attached with pins and combs.

The poodle cut
Hair cut to about four cm all over the head, then curled. Popular in the 1920s and 1950s.

Bob – 1920s–30s
New short hairstyle that caused a great sensation everywhere.

Permanent wave
This method of making hair curly using heat or chemicals was invented by Charles Nestlé in 1906.

The bouffant – 1950s
Came in as hats were going out of fashion – sometimes tinted with dye known as 'blue rinse'.

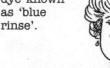

AT THE BARBER'S

Hedgehog (or Herisson) – 1790s
This effect could be achieved with natural hair or a wig – but not with a hedgehog.

Centre parting with dundrearies – 1800s
Side whiskers, also known as Piccadilly weepers, burnsides or sideboards.

Swallowtail beard – 1890
Double your stubble!

Van Dyck beard
Named after artist Sir Anthony van Dyck (1599–1641). Popular ever since (off and on).

Walrus moustache
Or soup strainer. 1860–70 and also 1915–30

Handlebar moustache
Popular with RAF pilots in WWII.

Marcel wave (with 'pencil' moustache) – 1920s
Wave created with hot irons – invented by Marcel Grateau, who had been a horse's groom!

Side parting (with toothbrush moustache) – 1930s. Popular with bossy types e.g. Adolf Hitler.

Crew cut
Also called varsity or G.I. Bob – 1940s onwards.

Goatee beards – Popular with arty types. 1940s onwards.

The Tony Curtis
Named after 1950s–60s film star and based on a Greek style.

A brand fit for hairos

The barbers of the early 20th century didn't put bear grease on their customers' hair but they did use the oily dressing known as Brylcreem. This was just the thing for controlling the slick 'n' smart "parted" hair fashions made popular by Hollywood film star heroes of the 1930s and 40s like Humphrey Bogart, Fred Astaire (and Mickey Mouse). The British government became completely convinced that a dollop of Brylcreem was absolutely essential to heroic performances so they issued it to the fighting forces during the Second World War and Royal Air Force pilots soon became known as the "Brylcreem boys".

The Brylcreem habit stuck. After the war the smashin' fashion fanatics of the 1950s continued to use it to keep their quiffs and "elephants' trunks" in place as they and their beehived, bouffanted girlfriends danced the jive to rock and roll music by stars who were making these new hairstyles so popular.

Something to do...

Two 1950s hairstyles that could go to your head
The "beehive"

This hairstyle was worn by pop stars of the late 1950s and early 1960s, such as Helen Shapiro and the Ronettes. It was really popular with wild teenagers (who were sometimes rather badly beehived!).

What to do

1 Lift up sections of your hair – probably about two or three hundred hairs at a time will be enough – you may count them if you wish but this is entirely up to you.

2 Still holding the ends of the hairs, comb the bunch from the top down towards your scalp until it forms a frizzy mass that more or less stands up on its own.

3 Repeat step two until the rest of your hair has been back combed (eyebrows optional) and it resembles an Old English sheepdog that's just had a really bad shock.

4 You are now ready to create the beehive shape itself. Do this by combing the frizzy outer layers of your hair smooth again, shaping your hair as you comb, until it forms a dome shape.

Buzzzzzzzzzzzzz

Style note one Team this hairdo with short socks, tight sweaters and skirts which have been stiffened with sugar and water. Chew bubble-gum and listen to "doo wop" records – but keep a sharp look-out for homeless bees at all times!

Style note two For boys who have just given themselves a beehive hairdo – this was the *girl's* section, so if you've just done your hair in this style *and* been out to the shops in it … tee hee! This one's yours …

The kiss curl
This style was made famous by 1950s rock 'n' roll star, Bill Hailey.

What to do

1 Wet a lock of hair from your fringe with water, soap, hair gel or spit.

2 Curl it into the shape of a letter "C".
3 Use your hand to press it against your forehead or cheek then hold it in place until it is completely dry and has set into the shape you require (the hair … not your forehead!).

4 Get kissed.

During the swinging 60s, greasy rock 'n' roll hairdos slipped right out of fashion and dry, natural styles quickly went …

Top of the crops

Number one **The Beatle cut**

This was a floppy, fringed style made mega-popular in the 1960s by The Beatles. It was a look that didn't need much styling or fiddling with – Beatles member, John Lennon, called it a hair *don't* … rather than a hair *do*. The style was also known as a *mop top*.

This was the longest hairstyle that European and American men had had since before the First World War and it marked the beginning of general world-wide male hairiness for at least the next ten years.

Number two **The Mod**

A fairly short, early 60s hairstyle, often with a very high parting. Had to look "dry", so definitely no grease or oil permitted! The hair was made to stand up by backcombing (like a 50s beehive) plus a few sneaky squirts of mum's hair lacquer. Pop singer Rod Stewart was famous for his *very* high back-combed mod hairdo in the 1960s, it was said to be at least 15 cm (six inches) tall (the hair … not Rod!). Girl mods have very

straight hair with a centre parting or long
"Cleopatra" style fringe, as worn by "mod" TV pop
show presenter Cathy McGowan.

Number three **The Afro**
In the 1940s and 50s, African Americans tried all
kinds of methods to straighten, or "conk" their hair,
including hot combs, grease and all sorts of nasty
chemicals to take out their natural curls. At last, in
the 1960s, the fashion started to change when a
band called The Jackson Five appeared on TV with
splendid bushy hairdos that showed off their
natural curls. Curls became cool with African
Americans, and soon white Americans wanted some
too. So lots of people started using all sorts of nasty
chemicals to try and curl their straight hair, and the
fashion for an Afro hairstyle soon spread around the
world.

Spiky hairdos – a few sharp facts
Punks didn't take orders from anyone about how
they should wear their hair ... they were just *wild*
about spiky hairdos like the Mohican and the
hedgehog. The Mohican was first worn by the native
American tribe of the same name and towards the
end of the Second World War, American

paratroopers had their hair cut Mohican-style for luck just before they were dropped into enemy territory in 1945.

In the 1970s, when the style became fashionable again, there wasn't much hair gel about, so punks had to keep their spikes in place with whatever they could lay their hands on, including margarine, toothpaste, washing-up liquid, soap and glue! After they'd arranged their hair into a suitably scary shape they dyed it really bright shades of red, green, purple and yellow using food colouring, spray paints or coloured powder. A member of the punk group, Generation X, said that his favourite haircare recipe was a mixture of orange juice, lemon juice and his own spit (uurgh!) while Sid Vicious of The Sex Pistols said he preferred to use egg whites on his (it's true ... no yolking!).

One person who wouldn't have been seen dead with one of those spiky punk hairstyles is the world-famous trendsetter who's the subject of our first...

Smashin' fashion style profile

Vidal Sassoon – British (b.1929)

So why's he so famous?

He's the hairdressing superstar who's had an enormous worldwide influence on hair fashion ever since the late 1950s. Someone once described him as "the man who did for haircutting what The Beatles had done for rock 'n' roll."

How did he get his smashin' career off the ground?

After learning his haircutting skills from the well-known 1950s hairdresser, Mr Raymond "Teasie-Weasie", Vidal set up business on his own in 1954.

But decided against having quite such a silly name as his old boss?

There was no need! News of his hairdressing talents spread quickly and fashion models and celebrities were soon adding *their* names to the list of famous people wanting to be "Sassooned". Many of the pop stars of the 1960s, like Sandie Shaw and Cilla Black, wore their hair in styles that Vidal had dreamed up.

What was the style that gave him his smashin' fashion breakthrough?

It was a natural-looking hairstyle called "the shape" which he introduced in 1959. It was styled to complement the wearer's face and sway around interestingly as they moved their head.

The perfect style for the swinging 60s then!

Absolutely! It was meant to be a big change from the old-fashioned, stiffly lacquered, 1950s bouffant hairdos which had stayed *perfectly still*.

Does anyone else rate him, apart from pop stars?

Not half! In 1963, the famous fashion designer, Mary Quant, began to get fed up with hair hanging down over the shoulders of the models who wore her clothes. So she went to Vidal and said, "Surely there is some other way to keep it away from their clothes?"

Why didn't she just get them to shave their shoulders?

Ho, ho! Vidal cut Mary's hair and that of her models in a style called the "bob" which had last been popular in the 1920s. His simple, natural looking hairstyles – a bit like Beatles cuts for girls – went perfectly with Mary's plain and uncluttered mini-skirts and skinny-rib tops.

What happened when the 60s stopped swinging?

WHERE AM I?

Like all fashion trendsetters, Vidal was always a step or two ahead of the times. During the 1970s he continued creating dozens of new styles including the "veil" cut. This was a popular style in which the hair was cut so that wispy strands fell around the wearer's face.

Is he still snipping?

No, Vidal hung up his scissors and retired from cutting during the 1970s. But he didn't retire from the world of hair fashion altogether. He has hairdressing salons and schools all over Europe and America and his team of stylists create "collections" of hairstyles – like the "wedge" cut – for each new season.

Last snip

Now that you know a bit more about smashin' hair fashions you might find it interesting to take a closer look at other people's hairstyles when you're out and about – but not *too* close though! You could try and work out what sort of fashion statements people are making, whether they're starting a retro revival of a great style from the past or if they are just stuck in a hair fashion time-warp. You may even develop the knack of spotting exciting never-seen-before hairstyles that are going to be the shape of things to come. Perhaps you've even taken a closer look at your own hairdo with a view to giving yourself a new image ... and then felt a bit disappointed, especially if you tried the DIY 1950s hairstyle and it went disastrously wrong? If that's the case, don't despair – quickly turn to the next chapter and choose a hat to hide it under.

NATTY HATS AND GORGEOUS GLOVES

Nowadays a lot of people think that wearing hats is a bit, well "old hat". But, up until about 50 years ago, most people were complete "hat heads", and didn't consider themselves to be properly dressed unless they were wearing some sort of head covering. Some people even wore hats in bed!

One of the reasons for all this hot-headed hat wearing was because what people wore on their heads was often an indication of their job or status. Hats said things like:

Occasionally headwear still does tell us about someone's power and responsibility.

Different types of hats can provide protection from dangerous or unpleasant things such as extremely hot sunshine, heavy falling objects, and missiles lobbed by your best enemies.

● Hats and headwear kept people warm while they were working in freezing fields, living in draughty hovels and castles, and wandering around the streets waiting for things like centrally heated shopping malls, schools, houses, cars and draught-proof stage coaches to be invented.

Hats generally meant so much to people that if someone came along wearing one that was a bit out of the ordinary, it could be *very* upsetting!

The terrifying top hat

In 1797 a hat seller called John Hetherington got himself a fabulous new bobby dazzler of a hat called a high silk or a topper. This trendy titfer was already all the rage in Paris but hadn't been seen in England. John thought he'd give everyone a treat by strolling around London wearing it and soon his new hat began to attract attention. People gasped and pointed, they stared in amazement, they grinned, they laughed and then they began to throw things at him!

Soon a small riot broke out – women screamed and fainted, a small boy had his arm broken in the crush – and then the police arrived. They hadn't come to arrest the rioters though ... they'd come to arrest John! He was taken before the magistrates and fined £50 for disturbing the peace ... just for wearing a hat! The charge was that he had:

...appeared on the public highway wearing upon his head a tall structure of shining lustre and calculated to disturb timid people.

One way or another, everyone in this story seemed to go completely over the top, but that's the effect smashin' fashion has on some people!

Top attitude

Eventually of course, the top hat became extremely popular. It was worn by the richest and most powerful men in the land. They obviously realized that a hat which was "calculated to disturb timid people", would come in really useful when it came to establishing their authority.

NOW GET DOWN THAT MINE, OR I'LL PUT AN EVEN BIGGER HAT ON!

Throw away fashion

While rich people wore large, expensive hats that told the world they were bigwigs (or just bigheads), poorer people wore hats that had a more practical purpose. They sometimes made their own hats out of paper – but these weren't party hats!

In the 19th century it was often extremely dirty and hot in the mills and factories where the poor worked and a lightweight paper hat was ideal to protect their heads and hair from dust and grime. Before starting the day's tasks, workers like carpenters, plasterers, plumbers and printers would make themselves a pillbox-shaped hat out of brown paper or yesterday's newspaper, and at the end of the day they would throw their hats away. Ready-made paper hats are still worn today by workers in places like bakeries and dairies, and in Italy bricklayers and builders still make their own disposable headgear.

Six hats that made the headlines

The hennin

The hennin hit the headlines long before the top hat. It was sometimes called a steeple head-dress (guess why!) and it was worn by women in the 15th century. It was said to have been first worn by Queen Isabella of France and was a popular fashion for nearly a hundred years. Hennins were often decorated with veils or ribbons and were meant to be worn so that no hair showed below them. Women who wore them plucked the hairs from the backs of their neck and foreheads so that they wouldn't be visible (the hairs, not the women). It is reported that some

I KNOW HOW TO GET AHEAD!

hennins were so tall that church doorways had to be altered to allow the wearers to get in.

AH! THEY'VE FINALLY GOT THE POINT!

The poke bonnet

This hat was said to have been designed in 1818 by Baroness Oldenburg to hide her (not particularly beautiful) face. The fashion caught on with beautiful as well as not so beautiful women. Even women from the Salvation Army Christian organization wore poke bonnets but it was reported that this was to protect their heads and faces from stones thrown at them while they were out preaching and collecting in rough areas of town!

GREAT! NO ONE WILL NOTICE MY BIG NOSE!

The bowler

I'M COMPLETELY BOWLERED OVER!

Up until the 1960s, this hat was a must for all businessmen, but strangely, it started out as a hunting hat and has never had anything to do with cricket, baseball or ten pins. It was made of hard material so the hunter was protected if he fell off his horse. Bowler was the name of the hat maker, but that's just its British name. In America it's called a derby, and in France it's called a melon!

The feathered hat

Trendy women at the end of the 19th century clamoured to get hold of these stylish hats with their fancy feather adornments. Hunters found that the easiest way to supply the feathers for this fashion was to catch the parent birds as they fed their young during nesting time and, as a result, thousands of chicks were left to starve to death. During the 1880s, in America alone, at least 5,000,000 birds were killed each year. Some species, like the egret and certain brilliantly coloured hummingbirds were almost wiped out. Whole birds were sometimes used as hat decorations. Eventually groups were formed to protest against this cruelty and at the beginning of the 20th century laws were passed to stop the trade in wild bird feathers.

The opera hat

This hat was a collapsible version of the topper. Some were made from rubber and others had a spring mechanism inside so that they could be conveniently flattened and stowed away under the seat when the owner was attending the opera. Some toppers also had pockets inside them – doctors kept their stethoscopes in theirs. Thieves used them to hide stolen goods in. One rogue – who'd stolen a pat of butter in a market place – hid it under his topper, but was later caught when it melted and dribbled down his face.

The baseball cap
The first baseball cap didn't actually have much of a brim at all but, in the 1930s, the American superstar baseball player, Babe Ruth (1895–1948), began wearing one with a big peak (to keep the sun out of his eyes). The peaked baseball cap eventually became *the* national headwear of America and was worn by everyone from presidents to pop musicians – who began wearing them in the 1970s and were later copied by fans all over the world.

Something to do...

Make your own hennin
What you need

- large sheet of thin card or thick paper
- scissors
- sticky tape
- glue
- a stapler (preferably long arm type)
- paints or felt-tip pens
- coloured ribbon
- paper strips or an old chiffon scarf

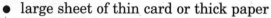

What to do

1 Cut your card diagonally in half and decorate it with felt-tips or paints.

2 Roll one of the triangles into a cone shape.

3 Stick loosely with pieces of sticky tape.

4 Trim the open end of the cone with the scissors so it slopes slightly.

5 Staple or glue the cone shape together. Note: if you want to decorate the hennin with a scarf or ribbons trap them in the seam first.

I FEEL A BIT POINTLESS

6 Wear it to school but first insist that the headteacher has all classroom doors raised by one metre.

Hat mad!

Did making your hennin leave you feeling a bit under the weather, or slightly peculiar? Hat manufacturers in the past used a poisonous chemical called mercuric nitrate to help mould felt (fabric made from wool and hair) into various hat fashion shapes. As well as bleaching the skin and damaging the kidneys of the people who worked in hat factories, constant use of this chemical also affected their brains, causing them to behave in all sorts of odd ways. Which is why people are still sometimes described as being *"as mad as hatters"*!

Smashin' fact

Fabrics sometimes have a textured surface which is known as the "nap". During Victorian times people wore a wide brimmed hat that was called the wideawake. This was because it was made from smooth material which ... "never had a nap!"

Now that you've finally stopped laughing at that hilarious 19th century hat joke you can begin reading about the fashion that's been on hand for absolutely ages ... the glove!

42

You may already know that gloves were probably first invented by primitive people as a way of keeping their hands warm during long cold winters (and to give their children something to lose on their way home from their friends' huts). And you probably also know that, as well as wearing gloves for warmth, people have also worn them:

● to protect their hands while they are working
● to protect their hands while they are playing
● to protect their hands while they are fighting
● to show everyone how rich and powerful they are ... and to make everyone else's hands look pathetic and inferior.

But did you know that gloves have often come in extremely handy in some much more unusual ways?

Some bygone uses for gloves

On the one hand some of these odd uses for gloves may be true ... but on the other, they may be false! Can you put your finger on the frauds?

1 When a landowner gave some of his land to someone else he would hand the new owner the title deeds (ownership documents) and one of his gloves! TRUE/FALSE

2 In Tudor times, if you discovered that a glove smeared in goose fat had been pinned to your front door during the night, it meant that the residents of your town or village suspected you of having "sticky fingers" (of being a thief). TRUE/FALSE

3 If someone slapped you in the face with their glove it meant that they wanted to fight you in a duel (if their hand was actually *inside* the glove when they slapped you, it meant that the fight had already started!). TRUE/FALSE

4 Gloves were used as part payment of rent. The records of a manor house in Nottinghamshire show that the annual rent was: one pound of cumin seed (a sort of spice), a steel needle, and a pair of gloves. TRUE/FALSE

5 Before beginning one of their famous marathon banquets, the ancient Romans often put on a pair of gloves. This would enable them to plunge their hands into 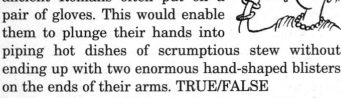 piping hot dishes of scrumptious stew without ending up with two enormous hand-shaped blisters on the ends of their arms. TRUE/FALSE

6 The Great Exhibition in London in 1851, drew crowds of people from all over the world. One London glovemaker hit on the idea of selling a glove with a map of the route to the exhibition printed on the palm. TRUE/FALSE

The language of glove

During the Middle Ages, a fashion trend began for using gloves as a sort of coded language. Rather than using words to say something, a person would just make a gesture with their glove and everyone would immediately know what they meant (but only if they spoke *glove*).

44

Some dos and don'ts of glove talk

1 You are in the presence of an enemy and you are wearing gloves. What is the worst thing you can do?

a) Bite your glove.

b) Bite your enemy's glove.

c) Stick the index finger of your glove up your enemy's nose.

2 You are on the bus. It stops outside Buckingham Palace and a member of the royal family gets on and sits next to you. They make small talk with you about the state of the weather and how hard it is to get good chambermaids, then express a wish to shake you by the hand. What must you do?

a) Spend the whole of your journey kneeling respectfully at their feet.

b) Report them to the conductor or driver because you've noticed that their bus pass is out of date.

c) Take off your gloves.

3 If you are approached in the street by some rough and uncouth person who looks as though they like nothing better than to cause trouble and they hurl their glove at your feet, what must you *not* do?

a) Mischievously run off with it and hide it on the glove counter of the nearest department store.

b) Say, "Excuse me, I think you dropped this?" then hand it back to them.

c) Stick it on your head and do your well known funky chicken impression.

4 You are making a promise which you definitely intend to keep such as telling your mum that you will wash the dishes, polish the cat and scrub the kitchen floor every Tuesday for the rest of your life. What must you do to prove that you are sincere?

a) Hand your mum a glove as you make the promise.

b) Solemnly pull on a pair of rubber washing-up gloves as you make your promise – then wear them for the rest of your life.

c) Wear a glove pinned on your chest to show that you have vowed with all your heart to devote your life to the service of others.

Answers:

1a) If you bite your glove in the presence of an enemy it means that you are swearing deadly vengeance upon them. In other words you are making a promise to kill them!

2c) If you keep your gloves on in the presence of royalty they will suspect that you are concealing a weapon in order to assassinate them and they will be most offended.

3b) If you return the dropped glove it means that you have just accepted their challenge to a fight to the death.

4a) Once you have handed over the glove it means that you have made a pledge that you can never go back on.

Five fascinating facts about gloves

1 In the town of Limerick in Ireland, gloves were made from the skin of unborn calves. The gloves

46

were so thin and delicate that they could actually be folded up and fitted inside empty walnut shells – they were often displayed like this in the shop windows of the town. They were obviously gloves for nut cases!

THESE WALNUTS ARE REALLY CHEWY...

2 That well-known queen of France (and all round untrustworthy person), Catherine de Medici (1519–1589), got her glovemaker to make gloves that were soaked in poison. She didn't wear the gloves herself – she gave them as gifts to people who annoyed her. The poison from the deadly gloves seeped out of the material and into the wearer's bloodstream through their skin, eventually killing them (as well as putting a welcome stop to their thumb sucking and nail-biting habits!).

3 Anne Boleyn, the second wife of King Henry VIII of England, was born with six fingers on one of her hands. Anne wasn't particularly proud of the fact that she had an extra finger so she got the royal glovemaker to design her a five-fingered glove that would conceal her spare pinkie. She then started a

THERE'S DEFINITELY SOMETHING ODD ABOUT HER – BUT I CAN'T PUT MY FINGER ON IT...

fashion for wearing gloves indoors so that she would have an excuse for hiding her extra digit (she'd already tried to start a fashion for having six fingers but somehow it just didn't catch on).

4 When the tombs of King Edward I and King John were opened, it was discovered that they'd been buried wearing gloves (very sensible, considering how nippy the night can get in those old stone crypts!).

5 In the 1920s fashionable women wore gloves that reached right up to their elbows – or sometimes even as far as their armpits. These gloves, which were made from the skin of young goats, often took up to 20 minutes to put on (it's true, no kidding!).

If it goes "Wuff!" ... it isn't a muff

If you're not keen on the idea of wearing gloves but you want to keep your fingers warm and be incredibly trendsetting at the same time, you could always go for an attractive hand cosy known as a muff. A muff is a sort of one piece glove with no fingers. It's a bit like a huge furry sausage roll ... but without the sausage!

If you'd never seen a muff before and saw someone wearing one you could be forgiven for thinking that they were cruelly walking around with their hands stuck up the opposite ends of a small and helpless furry animal.

Muffs used to be extremely fashionable with rich ladies and gentlemen who didn't have much to do with their time (or hands), and were hardly ever worn by working bricklayers, milkmaids or classical pianists.

Anyway that's quite emuff of that, ha, ha. Here's a really useful tip from Count Alfred Guillaume Gabriel D'Orsay (1801–1852). He was a French fashion designer, author, painter and sculptor and general raver about town. The Count said...

You should change your gloves at least six times a day.

(But always remember to give the receipt to the sales assistant when doing so!)

As the 20th century wore on, the fashion for wearing gloves wore off. People didn't need them so much – their homes were much warmer and they travelled about in heated buses and trains or in nice warm motor cars. Generally speaking, gloves were only worn when circumstances made it absolutely necessary, e.g. compulsory snowball fights, rose pruning, fumigating the cat's bottom. Then, in the 1980s a certain pop singer began appearing in public wearing black elbow-length gloves. Suddenly, gloves became a popular fashion item again, all because our next celebrity trendsetter had worn them at her concerts!

Smashin' fashion style profile

Madonna Louise Ciccone – American (b.1960)

ANYTHING YOU CAN DO ICON DO BETTER

Claims to fame?
Glove wearer, model, pop singer and 20th century fashion icon.

Fashion what?
Fashion *icon* ... that means she's a sort of symbol who represents all that is new and exciting in the world of fashion and pop. Her fans look to her for a lead and once she's done something a bit different and daring they follow suit.

Or glove?
Yes, got it in one!

So what's she done apart from making glove-wearing fashionable?
Oooh, lots! For starters ... she's worn her

Jean-Paul Gaultier designer underwear as outerwear...

Is she a bit absent-minded then?

Of course she isn't – she *wanted* to do it! She and Jean-Paul – the French designer who had the

undies idea – were making a sort of *"this underwear looks just great so let's show it off!"* fashion statement.

So did this "fashion statement" have much impact on the fans then?

Sure did! When they saw its startling effect they immediately copied it for themselves.

What else has she done?

She's appeared in skimpy tops and rolled down the waist band of her tube-shaped skirts so that lots of pop and fashion fans could get a glimpse of her bare midriff and marvel at her celebrity tummy button.

Madonna is full of smashin' fashion ideas isn't she?

That's right! Fashion and pop writers say that Madonna *"re-invents"* herself over and over again.

Re-whats herself?

Re-invents herself! It means that she frequently creates a whole new personal image by getting new clothes, new accessories, a new hairstyle, a new hair colour and new make-up.

It must be exhausting! Where does she get all her ideas from?

The history of fashion really! She assembles her outfits by dipping into different fashion eras then mixes and matches all sorts of styles in original and eye-catching ways – like long gloves from the 1920s, tight skirts from the 1940s, strings of pearls and beads from the 1950s, and lace tank tops from the 1960s. This pick 'n' mix approach to fashion is sometimes called *"style surfing"*!

How much influence has she had on fashion?

Lots! During the 1980s so many girls wanted to look like her that a clothing company called *"Madonna-wanna-be"* was started to supply them all with Madonna-type clobber.

There must have been mini-Madonnas everywhere?

There were!

BUT I THOUGHT YOU SAID "LET'S ALL DRESS UP AS MY DINNER"...

Last stitch

Regularly dreaming up a completely new image for yourself, as Madonna does, is what puts a lot of the fun into smashin' fashion. It's a way of using a bit of artistic flair to say something about yourself, just like painting, dancing, singing (and sulking?). You might like to follow the lead of trendsetters like Madonna or you might prefer to create a brand new look of your own...

FAB FASHION FOR YOUR FEET

Have you ever experienced the "new shoe" thrill? You know the feeling – you get a brand new pair of shoes that are just so perfect that all you want to do with them is:

a) wear them all the time and never take them off (even in bed), or

b) put them on a shelf and look at them, so they'll stay perfect for ever.

Don't worry, you're not alone ... for centuries shoes have been more than just a couple of convenient places to keep your feet. Over the years, people have been pretty weird about their footwear. They have:

● used shoes as good luck charms (especially at weddings)

● made up stories about magical shoes, like the ones in *Cinderella*, or *The Wizard of Oz*
● used shoes to change the way they look – elegant, graceful ... or taller. Most people use their shoes to protect their toes from grot, grime, heat, cold, rampaging tarantulas, clod-hopping carthorses ... and other people's shoes.

How well do you know your shoes?

Get off on the right foot by spotting the fake footwear in this quiz... Four of the following shoe styles are real but the other one has just been ... cobbled together!

1 Chopines These staggeringly spectacular shoes were worn by women in the Italian city of Venice.  The fashion originally started in the 16th century and just carried on growing and growing. Eventually, some women were staggering round on shoes which towered as high as half a metre (nearly two feet). The shoes got their great height from the enormous wooden blocks on which they were mounted. When the women went out for a "wobble" they had to be supported by a couple of servants. TRUE/FALSE

WE'RE ALL FALLING OVER OURSELVES TO GET THESE NEW CHOPINES!

SPLOSH!

2 Mukluks These boots are made from seal skin, moose skin or walrus hide. The hair is left on the skin and turned inside the boot for warmth. They are worn by North American Inuit people and are just the job for those freezing Arctic regions. Before the boots are made, Inuit women prepare the hide by giving it a really thorough chewing so that it's extra supple and comfortable! TRUE/FALSE

3 Piccadilly springers These
shoes were worn by the street
urchins of Victorian London. The
boys and girls – who were often very small –
survived by picking pockets, pilfering from market
stalls and jumping in and out of open windows on
the off-chance of stealing small valuables. In order
to give them the extra reach and height they needed
to carry out these activities, and to make good their
escapes in a series of startling bounds and bounces,
the waifs wore small boots with one or more power-
ful coiled metal springs built into the soles and
heels. The boots were known as Piccadilly springers
after the area of London where the children tended
to gather. TRUE/FALSE

4 Chinese "lotus" shoes These
strangely shaped shoes were worn
by Chinese women from the 11th
century to the beginning of the 20th century.

Throughout this time in China, *very* small feet were generally considered to be very attractive and fashionable. In order to achieve the tiny foot shape, girls had their feet tightly bound with bandages from a very early age. As a result they grew up with feet that were so deformed they were almost the shape of a lotus flower. TRUE/FALSE

5 Brogues Brogues are stout leather shoes worn by men and women. They are recognizable by  their distinctive wing-tip toes and the patterns of tiny holes which are picked out in their leather uppers. They were first worn by Irish gamekeepers and farmers who spent most of their working lives tramping around the damp and boggy Irish countryside. Holes were made in the brogues in order to let out the water which gradually seeped into them and as the wearers "waded while they worked" the water drained from the shoes. TRUE/FALSE

The "coolest" footwear in the world

If the people who lived in ancient civilizations like Egypt, Rome and Greece had worn old-fashioned brogues they would no doubt have found those drainage holes really useful for the sweat to pour out of – but the shoes would have been far too hot and uncomfortable for their climates. What they needed were shoes that would protect their feet from burning hot sand and pavements (plus the odd bad-tempered snake or scorpion), but also leave them comfortably cool and air conditioned – so what could be more perfect than a pair of sandals!

Four ways to "say it with sandals"

1 *How the ancient Greeks bared their soles to their loved ones*

If one ancient Greek gave another ancient Greek a cheeky smile and said, "I've got a crush on you!" they probably meant it. It was the custom of people living in ancient Greece to paint a picture of the person they loved on the soles of their sandals so that they were accompanied by the object of their affections wherever they went.

2 *How the ancient Egyptians "defeated" their worst enemies*

The ancient Egyptians had the opposite idea when it came to saying it with sandals. They painted a picture of their worst enemy inside their sandal sole. Once they had got the image of the hated person securely imprisoned inside their footwear they would grind them into the ground with every step they took.

3 *How to create a good impression*

Footloose and fancy free ancient Greek and Roman women who wanted to attract new boyfriends – and weren't too fussy about who they were as long as they had plenty of money – had the words "follow me" written in nails on the soles of their shoes. As they walked about looking ravishingly beautiful and casting flirtatious glances over their shoulders, the words would be printed in the sand. Hopefully, the rich and lonely men of their dreams would get the message and follow the trail.

4 *Footnotes for lost soldiers*

Roman soldiers often had the emblem or badge of their regiment marked out in nails on the soles of their sandals. These marks were probably used as a way of identifying which regiment a soldier belonged to – especially after he had "turned up his toes" following a fatal encounter with an enemy. They may also have proved useful if a soldier lost his regiment – he could look out for a trail in the sand and recognize the mark of his legion. All he would have to do then would be to follow the trail until he was reunited with his comrades.

WELL, THEY CAME THIS WAY ALL RIGHT...

Something to do ... if you dare!

How to make yourself a pair of ancient Greek or Egyptian sandals ... and have the coolest feet in your street!

What you need

- a fairly big piece of strong cardboard – about 30 cm (one foot) wide and 60 cm (two feet) long
- two pieces of ribbon, tape or string – each about

three metres (ten feet) long
- a pencil (between four–ten cms (1½–4 inches) in length
- scissors
- a piercing tool (*be **really** careful with this – get an adult to help you use it*)
- PVA glue

What to do

1 Take off your shoes and socks. Stand on the cardboard – open the window (phew … that's better). Draw around your feet.

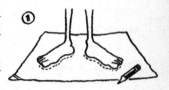

2 Cut out the shapes you have drawn and place them on the remaining piece of cardboard. Now draw round them again and cut out your next two foot shapes. You should now have two right soles and two left soles.

3 Place your feet on one pair of the soles – make a pencil mark between your toes:

4 Use the piercing tool to make a hole where the mark is on each sole. Take two pieces of your ribbon or string and thread the ends through the hole and firmly glue them to the back of the sole.

5 Make two more holes at

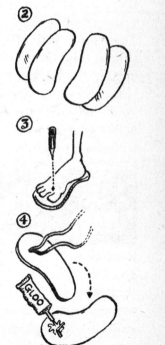

either side of the sole like this:
Thread the short length of
ribbon through the hole to
make a loop and then tie the
ends together at the back and
glue them down.

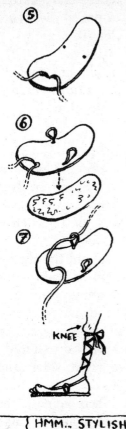

6 Cover the back of the sole in
PVA glue and stick the matching
sole to it. Put it under a weight
and let the glue dry (…you
should have taken your foot off
it by now). Start again to
finish the other shoe.

7 When the glue is dry, thread
the straps through the loops
you made like this:

Then put your foot on the
sandal and cross the straps
around the back of your ankle.
Now criss-cross the straps up
your leg and tie them just
below your knee.

KNEE

8 Conquer Gaul (optional).

HMM.. STYLISH
SANDALS!

Foot note
You could do as the ancient Greeks did, and decorate
your new footwear with a painting or drawing of
someone who is in some way special to you, like your
sweetheart, or your hamster (or yourself?).

It's "waterlooing" it down – *I think*
I'll put on me Wellesleys!

Someone who certainly gave his enemies a hard time was that tough old boot, Arthur Wellesley (1769–1852). Arthur was fond of travelling to foreign places, meeting people … and conquering them. This is what he did:

And he started a fashion for wearing the slim

63

leather riding boots that had become his trademark – or "wellingtons" as they soon became known!

As time moves on fashions change and memories fade. The name of an item of smashin' fashion often stays the same but its use and even its look can change completely.

Perhaps Arthur won the Battle of Waterloo because he got all his generals to stamp on his new boots? Shoes have always been associated with good and bad luck. So are you shoe-perstitious?

Five silly shoe-perstitions

1 When you go out in new shoes for the first time you must get your friends to tread all over them. This will bring you good luck (or completely flat feet?).

2 If your shoes squeak as you walk, it means that they've not been paid for (and that you've just set off the in-store security system).

3 If you see a white horse you must mark the sole of your shoe with a cross then say, *"White horse, white horse, bring me luck today or tomorrow."*

4 In Norfolk, England, people once believed that if

a girl put a clover leaf in her shoe she would marry the next man she met.

5 If your shoelace comes undone … it means that someone who fancies you is thinking about you at that very moment – probably something like, "Just look at that idiot, 11 years old and *still* can't tie his laces properly!"

Smashin' fact

Up until the 18th century there were no right and left fitting shoes, cobblers just made them to fit either foot – so people could stick their shoes on whichever foot they fancied (a tradition which many small school children continue to this day).

The shoes that were completely *cracows*!

In medieval times trendy people all over Europe became obsessed with wearing long, pointy shoes known as *cracows* or *poulaines*. Fashion victims of the Middle Ages went to ridiculous lengths to have the sharpest footwear in town. Can the following facts all be true ... or is someone just *poulaine* your leg?

1 The pointed-toe shoes first became trendy in Poland – as soon as other people saw them they thought that their own ordinary round-toed shoes were pointlessly old fashioned and the craze for *cracows* spread all over Europe. TRUE/FALSE

2 The fashionable footwear was called *poulaines* – after the old French name for Poland ... or *cracows* after the old Polish capital city. TRUE/FALSE

3 The points on some of the shoes were as long as 60 cm (two feet). TRUE/FALSE

4 Some of the points were so long and inconvenient that *poulaine* wearers had to walk upstairs backwards to avoid tripping over their trendy toes! TRUE/FALSE

5 When the craze reached its height it was said that a man wearing *poulaines* could be sitting in a tavern in Belgium with the toes of his shoes resting in a pizza parlour in Holland. TRUE/FALSE

6 In order to stop their *poulaines* flopping about the footwear fanatics fixed a little chain to the toes and fastened the other end to their knees or their waist. TRUE/FALSE

7 Some people stuffed grass, horsehair and dried moss into the ends of their *poulaines* then curled up the ends like a ram's horn. TRUE/FALSE

Answers: They're all TRUE – apart from **5** (obviously!).

Pointless foot note
Knights in the 14th century wore a sort of sharp, metal *poulaine* as part of their armour. Things got so crowded at the Battle of Sempach in 1386, that Austrian knights were forced to dismount from their horses in order to continue fighting. Once they were on the ground they found that their sharp toes got in the way and they had to quickly snap them off. And so they adopted a *"Snap, cracow ... and bop!"* approach to warfare.

Toff or not?

The rich and ruling classes relied on their "exclusive" fashions to set them apart from the "great unwashed" (as the common folk used to be known).

So whenever ordinary people pinched their fashion ideas …

… they would get upset and pass laws saying who could wear what – a bit like school uniform rules – but for the grown-up populations of whole countries! These laws are known as *sumptuary laws* and throughout the history of fashion (particularly between 1300–1800) governments have been making them – and sensible people have been generally ignoring them. Sumptuary laws were eventually passed to stop the spread of *poulaines* – this is what they said (…more or less!):

NOTICE
To all Grotty, Poor, Ordinary People
TOE THE LINE
OR ELSE!!

In England – No Person may wear shoes with toes that are longer than half a metre (19½ inches) – unless they have an income of more than forty pounds a year (and there's no chance of that … cos that's Mega Bucks to you lot!)

In Germany – No one can wear shoes with toes that are more than 60 cm (2 feet) long – apart from barons (… and people with really big feet)

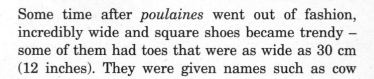

Some time after *poulaines* went out of fashion, incredibly wide and square shoes became trendy – some of them had toes that were as wide as 30 cm (12 inches). They were given names such as cow mouths, ducks' bills and bears' paws ... and they looked like this ...

... and then, just as people in England were beginning to have fun with this new smashin' fashion, the "fashion police" moved in again. This time, that old spoil sport, Queen Mary Tudor (1516–58), brought in a law to limit the width of those shoes to 15 cm (6 inches) – she was obviously very narrow minded!

Smashin' fashion note
When a trend suddenly disappears or dies out it is often replaced by a style that is its exact opposite – such as long skirts for short ones, tight ones for wide ones, big shoulders for narrow ones etc.

Smashin' fashion footwear tip

Never wear brown boots in London, unless you wish to earn the sneer of the footman.

Lady Troubridge (1866–1946), from her book on etiquette.

Final point

The fashion for pointy-toed shoes was revived in the late 1950s. This time they weren't called *poulaines* or *cracows* they were called "winkle-pickers". When they went out of fashion again, they were replaced with … more square-toed shoes called chisels or wedges (now, where has that happened before?).

The lumps of wood that beat the crud

Have you ever stood in something quite disgusting – no, *not* a classroom, something *far* worse than that – and then had to wipe it off your shoe? If you have, you'll be familiar with the problem that people in the Middle Ages had to put up with. The tracks and lanes of medieval Europe were all *incredibly* mucky. Going for a walk (particularly in bad weather) was more like going for a paddle through something that was a cross between a primeval swamp and a farmyard manure heap. If you were wearing your best new, cloth or leather *poulaines* or your crazy cow-mouths, they wouldn't stand a chance.

Round the clog protection

So that was what you did – you wore your trendy
shoes inside pattens, that is, you did if you were rich
enough! In medieval times poor people (usually from
country areas) generally couldn't afford leather or
cloth shoes so they just had to settle for wearing the

hollow blocks of wood on their own. The wooden shoes, or *clogs*, as they came to be called, were very hardwearing, and suited the rough, tough lifestyle of the country people (down to the ground).

Clog style-file

Although clogs were extremely hardwearing they weren't particularly comfortable or warm. On cold winter days, perhaps when a blizzard was blowing and the peasants were wandering round the countryside looking for a twig to put on their fire, they would stuff straw or moss inside their clogs for comfort and warmth (those medieval country folk certainly knew how to pamper themselves, didn't they?).

WELL, MY CLOGS ARE TOASTY WARM, BUT I CAN'T FIT MY FEET IN...

But clogs have been worn in Europe and eastern countries for centuries and even today they're used for everyday wear in some places – factory workers in Scandinavia still wear clogs for work. And in Belgium and Holland children put out a clog for Father Christmas instead of a stocking.

Smashin' fashion footwear tip

If you have new shoes which hurt as you walk, do as some 19th century toffs did, and get a servant (your little brother or sister?) to wear them for about six months. After this the shoes will be really supple and comfortable (not to mention out of fashion and probably completely worn out).

Smashin' fashion goes shopping for shoes and boots

WOMEN'S DEPARTMENT

Pantofles – late 16th century.

COLOURED STOCKING

CORK SOLE

Satin 'mules' – first designed to be worn in the bedroom.

SILK FRILL

NO BACK

HEEL

Victorian ladies' ankle boot – 1883 – made in factories, not hand-stitched by a cobbler.

BLACK SILK

LACES WITH TASSELS

COLOURED STITCHING

Velvet and lame evening slipper – 1922 – Designed by André Perugia (1898–1976).

Suede boots with monkey fur trimming – made by Perugia for fashion designer Elsa Schiaparelli (1896–1973). He also made her a hat shaped like a high-heeled shoe.

Ruby slippers – worn by Judy Garland in the film *The Wizard of Oz*. Eight pairs were made in 1938, including small ones for close-up shots. One pair sold for $165,000.

Invisible shoes – created in 1947 by Salvatore Ferragamo (1898–1960). He dreamed up over 20,000 different shoe styles!

SUEDE HEEL

SEE THROUGH PLASTIC TOP

MEN'S DEPARTMENT

Cavalier or 'bucket' boot – 1600 – ladies were said to admire a 'good wrinkle' in a chap's boots.

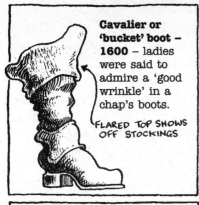

FLARED TOP SHOWS OFF STOCKINGS

'Red heeled' shoes – 1670s – worn by King Louis XIV of France.

JEWELLED BUTTERFLY-BOW BUCKLE

18cm (5 ins) RED HEEL

TINY PAINTINGS OF BATTLES.

D'Orsay pump – 1820s – Named after Count D'Orsay who designed them.

V SHAPED DIP ON EITHER SIDE

Hunting 'Blucher' or 'Derby' – 1885 – named after another general who fought with Wellington at the Battle of Waterloo.

Balmoral – 1925 – named after a royal estate – made popular by Queen Victoria's husband.

Black and white Oxford brogues – 1913 – popular with golfers, who added spikes to the soles.

Beetle crushers or carpet creepers – 1950s – Worn by rock 'n' rollers and 'teds'.

BLUE SUEDE

← THICK CRÉPE SOLE

Walking on air

Having shoes that are comfortable is really important – especially if you've got damaged feet. After breaking  his foot in a skiing accident in 1945, a German doctor called Klaus Maertens found his ordinary shoes far too uncomfortable to wear so he designed himself a pair of boots with "air cushioned" soles – the soles had pockets of air built into them, rather than being completely solid.

These boots eventually became known as Doc Martens or DMs and were adopted as smashin' fashion footwear by teenagers from the 1960s onwards. Since then they've been produced in all sorts of colours and styles.

Smashin' fact

The Dalai Lama (the spiritual leader of Tibet) and Pope John Paul II are both Doc Marten fans. The Pope wears his for work and when he goes hiking. He likes them so much that he placed an order for 100 pairs – they weren't all for him though, he wanted a few pairs for his helpers as well.

Fashion shoes that will run and run

Adolf Dassler originally designed his canvas track shoes for top sports stars like the world record breaking athlete Jesse Owens (1913–80). In the 1940s it was decided that running shoes should be made much stronger, so that they could withstand the pounding they were given by athletes. Three strips of leather were added to them and the first trainer was born. Adolf's shoe companies later became known as Adidas and Puma and their shoes – are still running!

Trainers have been successful because...

a) they're comfortable ... *and*

b) to many people, they're the last word in great-looking foot fashion.

As well as putting a spring in your step, a well-made pair of trainers can protect your feet from hard knocks – they may even help you to win races, or run away from people you want to avoid. But, if they happen to be trendy designer trainers, they can also land you in trouble...

Smashin' fact
In April 1983, 20-year-old Alfred E. Acree was running away from the police in Charles County, Virginia, USA. The police were anxious to talk to him about some illegal activities he'd been involved in, but Alfred wasn't in the mood for a cozy chat so he ran off into some woods. It was night time and absolutely pitch dark but the

police had no problem catching him – he was
wearing a pair of "Light Gear" trainers – the sort
that have little lights built into the heels. As he
bounded along the forest paths his trendy
trainers told the cops exactly where he was.

"Fashion is more powerful than any tyrant" – *Old Latin proverb*

Someone else who's got at least one pair of shoes
that light up in the dark is Imelda Marcos. Imelda
and her husband, Ferdinand, the late President of
The Philippines, ruled their country with a rod of
iron and didn't let anyone get in the way of their
quest for wealth and power. Imelda may have
resisted her political opponents quite successfully
but when it came to a snazzy pair of smashin'
fashion shoes she just couldn't say "No!". She's said
to have collected a total of 2,600 pairs of them!
That's enough shoes to be able to wear a new pair
every single day for seven years. Her collection
includes trainers made from alligator skin (very
snappy!), pumps covered in gold leaf, and disco
shoes with rechargeable batteries and flickering
lights. Whenever she flew abroad on diplomatic

trips with her husband she had her clothes sent in a separate jumbo jet!

OH, AND WHILE I'M HERE I'LL TAKE A MILLION GALLONS OF SHOE POLISH AND 5,200 ODOUR-EATERS...

One pair of shoes Imelda didn't get her hands on was worn with a little bit of difficulty by supermodel Naomi Campbell, in 1993. They were bright blue, fake crocodile-skin, platform-soled shoes. And they were created by Vivienne Westwood who is the celebrity designer currently tottering down the Smashin' Fashion Catwalk of Fame ...

Smashin' fashion style profile

Vivienne Westwood – British (b.1941)

Claim to fame?
Fashion designer – often thought to be *rather* outrageous! She was once described as a "pioneer of street style" but has never actually designed a street.

Did she start her working life in the fashion biz?

No, she trained as a teacher but soon decided she'd be much happier working in the fashion industry.

So how did she get her smashin' fashion career on the road?

By putting her fashions on the road … the King's Road in London, where she opened a shop in 1971. This was a really good move 'cos the King's Road had been incredibly popular with fashion victims since the early 60s. They would flock there in their thousands to pose around in what became known as "The Saturday Parade".

What sort of smashin' fashions did she sell?

Lots of clothes made out of leather and rubber and decorated with safety pins, zips and studs.

It wasn't a school outfitters then?

It certainly wasn't! Vivienne wore these sorts of clothes herself, and during the 1970s they became incredibly popular with punks.

And did she do this all on her own?
No, she had a partner called Malcolm McLaren who also happened to be the manager of the punk rock group, The Sex Pistols. In 1983 Malcolm noticed that there was a link between trendy clothes and pop music.

After everyone else had realized it in 1956?
That's right, he said that when a pop group signed a contract with a record company they should have "*£1,000 a week to spend on clothes*". He also said, "*As long as a group has the right look today ... the music doesn't matter too much.*"

So that's how "Take That" got away with it!
Take *who*?

What did she do next?
When punk went out of fashion in the 1980s, she launched her "new romantic" look to replace it. She designed things like huge swirling petti-  coats, outrageous ruffles and enormous baggy boots (and that was just for the fellas!).

So, what's this story about the shoes then?

In 1993, the supermodel, Naomi Campbell, was modelling a Vivienne Westwood outfit that included those extra high, bright blue, platform-soled shoes. When she was part way along the catwalk Naomi lost her balance and fell on her bottom.

Maybe she suffered an attack of dizziness brought on by her tremendous height?

Quite possibly. After all, comfort and convenience have never been fashion's strong points, have they? But those shoes are history now.

You mean we should forget about them?

No, they're an historical exhibit at the Victoria and Albert Museum in London (in a locked glass case with a health and safety warning?).

Smashin' fashion statement

"There's never a new fashion but it's old." – Geoffrey Chaucer (c. 1340–1400). History repeats itself, that's what Chaucer was saying. And it's true! Vivienne Westwood's platform shoes looked wild and new and different, but the idea was ancient! It came, of course, from those potty *chopines* of the 16th century.

EYE-CATCHING ACCESSORIES

Your hair is the cat's whiskers, your feet are the bee's knees (well, almost) and you're about to get togged up in some terrific tops and brilliant bottoms that might turn out to be the cat's pyjamas. But fashion isn't all clothes, shoes and hairdos. All kinds of other extra items have been classed as fashionable at one time or another and it's accessories that can give your look that final sparkle. Most of the eccentric accessories in this chapter were essential fashion items once upon a time.

Seventeenth century face fashion

In the 17th century, trendy European women became completely stuck on the fashionable bits and pieces known as patches. Their clothes weren't threadbare or anything – they didn't patch *them* – they patched their faces! Why do you think they did this?

a) In days gone by people aged very rapidly. Women's skin was nowhere near as tough as it is nowadays. Due to the effects of the elements – the sun, wind and rain, their cheeks, chins and foreheads quickly wore out and were often in need of repairs.

b) Patches were a stylish way to decorate your face – and brilliant for hiding nasty scars left over from hideous illnesses, like smallpox.

c) Seventeenth century women were an incredibly rough lot. They were forever fighting and getting involved in duels about the ownership of dogs, children and boyfriends. As a result their faces were always full of rips and tears. They covered these up with patches which they carried about with them in handy kit form – a bit like modern day puncture repair kits.

Answer: b) The patches were worn by women and some men, too. They were first used as a way of covering up unsightly spots and blemishes due to smallpox or the plague etc. After a while, lots of women began to like the idea of looking like walking fuzzy-felt pictures and the fashion soon caught on. A whole variety of interesting shapes became available, ranging from modest circle, star and moon shapes for the less adventurous patcher to more elaborate shapes, like a coach and horses design (which was popular as a forehead decoration!).

YOUR PATCHES AREN'T A PATCH ON MY PATCHES

All that glitters

One set of accessories that has always been in fashion is jewellery. Even when clothes weren't much more than a body wrap, many men and women wore fabulous jewellery. But it usually had a purpose. OK, so it probably didn't keep you warm, or protect you from rain and sunshine, but it could show how wealthy you were, whether or not you were married, which clan you belonged to and it could have even more practical purposes too.

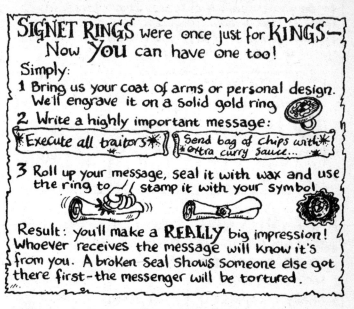

SUICIDE RING: *Things not going your way? Just been captured by your worst enemy and about to be force-fed to his sabre-tooth tortoises?* **DON'T** *die a slow, lingering death at the hand of your your foe.* **NOW** *you can die a swift and efficient death at the hand of... yourself!*

Secret compartment contains deadly poison

One bite and you're DEAD

URk!

ASSASSIN'S RING: THAT LION DESIGN DOESN'T JUST LOOK GREAT — IT'S DEADLY TOO! SIMPLY:

1 SELECT YOUR VICTIM

2. GIVE THEM A GRIN

3. SHAKE THEM FIRMLY BY THE HAND

CLAWS CONNECT TO POISON CAPSULE

AAAAAAARGH!

WARNING: AVOID SCRATCHING HEAD, BOTTOM ETC. AT ALL TIMES...

SQUEEZE HARD TO RELEASE POISON INTO ENEMY'S BLOODSTREAM

GAMBLER'S RING —

"MIRROR MIRROR ON MY RING

WHO IS GOING TO DEAL THE KING?"

If you're useless at cards then this ring's for you! Ingenious mirrored design is perfect to reflect action

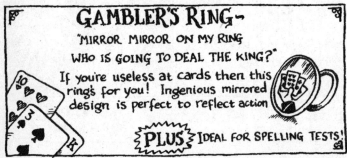

PLUS IDEAL FOR SPELLING TESTS!

Three sparkling gems of wisdom
The Victorian "jet" set

If you'd been unlucky enough to attend a Victorian funeral (and children often had to go) you might have received a rather unusual present. It was the fashion in those days to give each guest at a funeral a small piece of black jewellery made from coal! It was a special type of coal though, called jet. This was called mourning jewellery. It came in a variety of hideous styles, such as:

1 a necklace with a skull and crossbones pendant dangling from it, or

2 a finger ring with a skeleton motif.

Worst of all, you'd be expected to wear it for several months after the funeral to prove just how much you missed old thingumajig who had died.

Pearls of wisdom

Strings of pearls have been fashionable for centuries. But have you any idea what they actually are? They're made by shellfish, such as mussels, clams or oysters. If a grain of sand gets into the shell, the shellfish can't fish it out, 'cos it doesn't have any fingers. Instead, it squirts sticky stuff, called nacre, at the intruder, and the nacre starts to form a grey-white shiny ball. This is the pearl.

Strangely enough, if you don't wear your pearls very often, they could turn back into a sticky mush again – they like a bit of contact with your skin, so give yours an affectionate cuddle right now!

A jewel of an idea

Take another look at the enormous diamond encrusted ring that your teacher is wearing in his nose. Want to know a secret? It's not real ... it's a fake (the *ring*, not his nose!). Lots of the jewellery that is worn nowadays is not actually made with real jewel stones. The fake stones are made from a sort of glass paste which glitters just like the real thing. Paste copies of jewels – called "costume jewellery" – were first made in the 18th century as a way of fooling thieves into thinking that the rings and necklaces they were snatching from fashionable and wealthy travellers were the real thing.

A DAZZLING ARRAY OF JEWELLERY ~ FROM ANCIENT TO MODERN...

LIP PLATE – WORN BY MEN AND WOMEN AROUND THE WORLD, E.G: IN CHAD, ETHIOPIA AND SOUTH AMERICA

THAT'S ENOUGH OF YOUR LIP!

HUMAN SKULL – REPORTED TO BE WORN AS NECK JEWELLERY BY WIDOWS ON PITCAIRN ISLAND IN THE PACIFIC. 18TH CENTURY. THE HEADS BELONGED TO THEIR DEAD HUSBANDS...

HE ALWAYS WAS A BIT BONE-HEADED!

CELTIC BROOCH— AD 700. STYLISH— AND USEFUL FOR FASTENING CLOAKS, TUNIC, ETC.

BRONZE

WATCH RING 15th CENTURY LID OPENS TO REVEAL BIBLE SCENE...

RING →

→ BUILT IN ALARM

IT WAS AHEAD OF ITS TIME!

THE DRAKE JEWEL QUEEN ELIZABETH 1st GAVE THIS TO SIR FRANCIS DRAKE IN 1588 FOR DEFEATING THE SPANISH ARMADA...

AND IT'S GOT A PICTURE OF ME INSIDE

COR! TA!

TIE PIN AND BROOCH CONTAINING **HAIR** AND **TEETH.** VICTORIANS WERE FOND OF WEARING JEWELLERY CONTAINING A BIT OF THEIR SWEETHEART...

LOCK OF HAIR

DISCARDED TOOTH →

HAT PINS - EARLY 19th CENTURY. HELD HATS IN PLACE. DECORATED WITH FROGS, BEETLES, GRASSHOPPERS ETC.

HOLD STILL! THERE'S A BUG ON YOUR HAT!

BUT...

GOLD PLATED MICKEY MOUSE BROOCH WITH 2,000 CRYSTAL STONES...

AS WORN BY SUPERSTARS, INCLUDING MICHAEL JACKSON, OPRAH WINFREY AND ELIZABETH TAYLOR...

"THE EYE OF TIME" BROOCH— DESIGNED BY ARTIST SALVADOR DALI...

GIVE IT TO YOUR ONE TRUE LOVE— IF YOU NEED TO KEEP AN EYE ON THEM!

STRINGS OF **COLOURED GLASS BEADS.** WORN BY WOMEN OF THE SAMBURU TRIBE, KENYA, AFRICA. IF THEY AREN'T WEARING AT LEAST 2 KILOS THEY AREN'T PROPERLY DRESSED!

NECK RINGS - WORN BY WOMEN IN BURMA, ASIA. THEY START WITH 5 RINGS AS CHILDREN AND WORK THEIR WAY UP TO AS MANY AS 24...

THEIR NECKS SOMETIMES STRETCH TO MORE THAN 38CM (13 INCHES)

Bizarre bits and bobs

In 1854 an American writer called Henry Thoreau (1817–1862) wrote:

> *Every generation laughs at the old fashions but follows religiously the new.*

As circumstances in society change, so fashion accessories come and go – items that one generation considered terrifically trendy are later considered totally weird. Take a look at these once popular accessories from the dumpbin of time and see if you think they might come back into fashion.

The pomander

Here's an idea that's well past its smell-by date. In the 16th century when sewage flowed freely through the streets an ingenious new fashion promised to sweeten your nostrils. The pomander was first of all a hollowed-out orange, but later designs were hand crafted from silver and gold. It was filled with a generous dollop of perfume and hung around the neck.

ACTUALLY, I QUITE LIKE THE SMELL OF POO – BUT I CAN'T STAND THE PONG OF HIS POMANDER!

Plumpers

In the 17th century it wasn't unusual to feel down in the mouth. Lost teeth and tooth decay left many people with sunken cheeks. Fast-action plumpers were lightweight cork balls that were perfect for cheering up collapsed cheeks.

Before: *After:*

Crucial "nitwear" – the flea-trap

In the 17th century even the smartest of people were troubled with nits – they needed an insect deterrent that was a fashion accessory too.

Smashin' fashion style profile

George Bryan Brummel – British (1778–1840)

A smashin' fashion fanatic who was wild about fashion accessories was the 18th

century style victim, George Bryan Brummel –
but you can call him "Beau". Beau was what is
known as a dandy or a fop – that's someone who
is so obsessed with fashion that their whole life
revolves around it. He
was a real trendsetter
of his day and even
the future King of
England came to him
for fashion tips…

Beau was particularly nuts about cravats and
started a fashion for wearing them tied in large
and complicated knots ("Beau" ties?). His own
cravat had to be absolutely perfect before he
would even step out of his front door. If he didn't
manage to tie it perfectly first time he would sniff
haughtily and toss it to one side, pick up another
one and start all over again – even if it meant
spending all morning just tying cravats (… and
sniffing haughtily). And this was all because he
wanted to give everyone the impression that he'd
just "thrown on" the first cravat that came to
hand then knotted it in seconds.

In addition to being nuts about accessories like
cravats, Beau introduced some revolutionary
men's fashion ideas such as wearing *clean*
clothes … and having a really good *wash* before
you put them on. Before Beau came along, most
fashionable men thought that grooming was
something you did to animals – the idea of
actually being clean came as something of a
surprise to most of them.

⌐TEN TOP TIPS FROM AN ELEGANT EXPERT⌐

① To keep your skin clean and white, bathe in milk. I do it all the time. People tell me I've got the creamiest complexion in London!

② Before putting on your clothes in the morning, spend at least two hours scrubbing your skin with a stiff brush.

③ Don't have your clothes laundered in grotty, grimy, stinky old London. Do as I do...and send them away for refreshing weekend breaks in the country, where the air is pure and brooks babble with water that is as fresh as a... country brook!

④ Always use a servant to polish your shoes. They always scream and struggle a bit, but the super shine is worth the inconvenience.

⑤ Insist that your servant polishes the soles and heels of your shoes as well as the uppers. This will enable you to "show a clean pair of heels" when you're running away from people you owe money to... like I do!

⑥ I suggest that your servants polish your shoes with my special honey and champagne shoe-cleaning mixture. My valet will send you the recipe on receipt of a £50 note. USEFUL TIP: If the servants make a really good job of the polishing let them take the leftovers home for tea.

⑦ When you're finally ready to go out, have your sedan chair brought right into your front hall so that your perfect shoes are not touched by even one speck of dirt and not one hair of your immaculate hairdo is blown out of place.

⑧ If you meet a lady in the street Do NOT raise your hat to greet her — if you do you won't be able to return it to your head at that perfect jaunty angle that it took you so long to achieve.

⑨ Be fussy about your gloves. My glovemaker makes excellent glove fingers, but when it comes to the other bits he's all fingers — but definitely not thumbs. So I have those made by another glovemaker.

⑩ Take three hairdressers into the barber's shop... like me! I have one hairdresser for the fringe, one for the sides and one for the back.

JUST A TEENSY BIT OFF THE TOP, PLEASE...

The fantastic fan

Beau was not known to have been a committed fan carrier but he no doubt spent many happy hours in the company of women who were. Fans have been popular fashion accessories for centuries, particularly in hot countries, because you can use them to...

- Cool the air by wafting the fan about to create a breeze.
- Protect yourself from the glare of the sun.
- Protect yourself from insects like wasps and mosquitoes.
- Get fires started by "fanning" the flames.
- Let everyone know that you are really important by getting other people to do your wafting for you.
- Send coded messages of love to people you *fan*cy.

No one's exactly sure how the fan came into being but one old Chinese legend says it happened like this:

Warning: This old Chinese legend may just be a lot of hot air – it's probably more likely that fans developed from people's habit of cooling themselves with whatever large, flat object was to hand e.g. a palm leaf, a frying pan, a large lizard recently squashed by a hippopotamus.

Something to do

Make your own fantastic folding fan
What you need
- a length of thin paper (e.g. greaseproof or tracing paper) about 40 cm × 70 cm (15½ × 27½ inches)
- felt-tips, paints or crayons
- PVA glue
- two thin sticks about 45 cm (17½ inches) long – such as green garden canes or wooden kebab skewers (remember to remove kebabs from skewers before using).

What to do
1 Decorate your fan paper first – fans can look really great if you take some time and trouble to decorate them – using felt-tips, paints or crayons. Alternatively, put the paper over the top of some lace and make a pattern by rubbing a crayon over it.
2 Fold the piece of paper into pleats or strips about 2 cm (¾ inch) wide – keep folding until you end up with a wedge of paper like this:

3 Glue one end strip of the wedge then fold it in

half and glue the two halves of the strip together
like this:

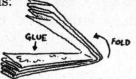

Glue one stick to each of the
edges of the paper – trim the
sticks so that they are the same
length as the edges like this:

Serious safety note If you do
use wooden kebab skewers,
remember to trim off the sharp pointed ends.
4 Go somewhere warm
and get wafting!

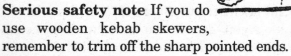

How to flirt with a fan
In terribly polite 18th and 19th century European
society, a young woman and young man weren't
usually allowed to speak to one another. To over-
come this problem the language of the fan developed
and became so popular that a Spaniard, appro-
priately named Fenella, actually published a set of
50 directions on how to speak "fan". Here are a few
you could try:
1 Carrying the fan in
front of your face
means, "Follow me!"

2 Twirling the fan in your left hand means, "We are being watched."

3 Drawing the fan through your hand means, "I hate you."

4 Drawing the fan across your cheek means, "I love you."

Why not try making up your own fan language – after all, it's fan to talk!

Some other fashion accessories that people used to keep cool during hot weather were umbrellas and parasols.

A wet weather fashion extra

Funnily enough, before the 18th century, umbrellas had nothing at all to do with wet weather. But in 1750 a man called Jonas Hanway had the inspired idea of using an umbrella to keep himself dry during a rainstorm – when people in the street saw him using a sun-shade to protect himself from the downpour they just couldn't believe their eyes.

In London, horse-drawn cab drivers were particularly upset when they saw what Jonas was doing and decided that they just weren't going to put up with this ridiculous umbrella fashion. They shouted insults at him, they jeered and they hooted, but Jonas ignored them.

Why were the cab drivers so upset about Jonas's umbrella fashion?

a) Their horses were so alarmed by the sight of the open umbrella that they all immediately sat down in the middle of the street and refused to move.

b) Many people used horse-drawn cabs as a way of avoiding sudden showers of rain. If the umbrella caught on, the cab drivers would lose a lot of business.

c) The drivers worried that absent-minded passengers would leave umbrellas in their cabs and they'd have to spend all their spare time returning them.

Answer: b) The cab drivers thought that the widespread use of umbrellas would ruin their business.

OK, so you might not feel especially trendy fluttering your fan, or flaunting your flea-trap or brandishing a brolly at the local disco, so it might be a better idea to kit yourself out with something really trendy and up-to-the-minute. Why not try some of these...

MOBILE PHONE — DOESN'T HAVE TO WORK... USE TOY ONE AND SAY "CIAO", "YAR" AND "SOOPER" EVERY FEW WORDS...

WALKMAN-TYPE CD OR CASSETTE PLAYER - BUT YOU DON'T ACTUALLY HAVE TO LISTEN TO IT...

POSING PENS— MONT BLANC, PARKER OR SCHAEFFER. IF YOU CAN'T AFFORD THE WHOLE THING JUST HOOK A PEN TOP OVER YOUR POCKET

SHADES (NEVER CALL THEM SUN-GLASSES) WEAR THEM AT ALL TIMES, ESPECIALLY IN THE DARK, AND IN BED.

A ROLEX WATCH— OR A CHEAP IMITATION - CHOOSE ONE WITH DIALS TO SHOW THE TIME OF DAY ALL ROUND THE WORLD SO YOU NEVER KNOW WHICH FACE TO LOOK AT

IMPRESSIVE CAMERA EQUIPMENT MUST HAVE STRAPS WITH TRENDY NAMES ON TO SLING AROUND YOUR NECK

SPORTS EQUIPMENT IN POSH CASES WITH HUGE NAMES ON — SAVE MONEY BY NOT BUYING THE EQUIPMENT

A LAP-TOP COMPUTER - HAMMER AWAY ON THIS IN THE SCHOOL DINING HALL, BUT KEEP YOUR ARM CURLED ROUND IT SO NO ONE CAN SEE WHAT YOU'RE WRITING...

IF YOU CAN'T AFFORD A FLASH GERMAN CAR, A FLASH GERMAN CAR KEYRING IS THE NEXT BEST THING...

CARRIER BAGS FROM TOP FASHION SHOPS - ASK FOR ONE WHEN YOU BUY YOUR PEN TOP

Be sure to make the most of your smashin' fashion accessories while you can. Don't forget, fashions fly by in a flash – this year's trendy trimmings will become ridiculous rubbish in no time at all! The next chapter might give you an idea of how it all happens...

TOPS, BOTTOMS AND CHANGING SHAPES

Designers are forever dreaming up weird and wonderful ways to change the way we look. But you might well wonder where all these new ideas come from? In the 20th century especially, a lot of fashion has been designed to shock poor old parents. But often famous people and events in the news can have a hand in the change. Even a war can make a huge difference to your choice of clobber. Five hundred years ago, just one punch-up between a couple of armies is said to have changed smashin' fashion all over Europe – from top to bottom.

A ripping yarn

1 In 1476, an army of Swiss mercenaries had a huge battle with Charles the Bold, Duke of Burgundy and his French soldiers, at Nantes in France.

2 After the battle the Swiss soldiers were all looking a bit the worse for wear – torn shirts, holes in trousers, shoelaces undone, heads missing etc.

3 They decided to spruce themselves up a bit. So they patched and mended their clothes with bits of the tents, flags and banners that the untidy French soldiers had left on the battlefield.

4 The Swiss didn't have their sewing kits with them, so they stuffed the bits of tent and banner inside their ripped clothing.

5 When the soldiers returned from the battlefield in their slashed and stuffed uniforms people were impressed.

6 Without going to the bother of fighting a battle, they knocked up some snazzily ripped outfits of their own.

The fashion didn't just apply to shirts, dresses and tunics, even shoes and tights got the slash treatment. The clothes that were worn underneath the ripped article would be pulled through, and the tears delicately embroidered.

The soldiers had accidentally sparked off a stunning new fashion idea that was to be popular in Europe until the middle of the 16th century – when people decided it had all been a bit of a rip-off.

The picture of 16th century chic

That trendy Tudor – King Henry VIII (1491–1547) – was the very model of a slashin' fashion fan. In this portrait painted by the German artist, Hans Holbein (1497–1543), the stylish sovereign is looking superb from top to toe in...

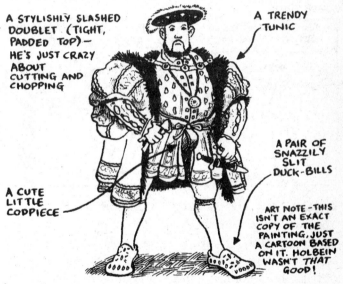

A STYLISHLY SLASHED DOUBLET (TIGHT, PADDED TOP) – HE'S JUST CRAZY ABOUT CUTTING AND CHOPPING

A TRENDY TUNIC

A PAIR OF SNAZZILY SLIT DUCK-BILLS

A CUTE LITTLE CODPIECE

ART NOTE – THIS ISN'T AN EXACT COPY OF THE PAINTING, JUST A CARTOON BASED ON IT. HOLBEIN WASN'T *THAT* GOOD!

Important fashion note – the "cod-piece"

No readers – trendy Henry *hasn't* tucked a tasty fish supper into the top of his tights in case he gets a bit peckish. Cod-pieces were a sort of bag that 15th and 16th century men wore in the spot where modern chaps keep their Y-fronts. There was a fashion for very short tunics at the time – and a cod-piece provided perfect protection for a man's more private parts.

Kings and queens of style

In times gone by, members of the royal family were considered to be the style setters of their day. Courtiers – that's other rich people who were closely associated with royalty (or creeps and toadies, as some people prefer to call them) – copied everything their bosses wore. Things have certainly changed since then!

Squeeze, then say "Cheese!"

You can learn a lot by studying old photographs and paintings like the one of Henry. But isn't it funny how people in paintings are often wearing smashin' outfits, but looking thoroughly miserable? The old clothes look stylish, but were often unbelievably heavy and uncomfortable to wear. And worse were the bits of the outfit you can't see in the painting. You'll probably never know whether Henry had something underneath his costume to trim him down to size.

Fashion has an irritating habit of telling us what shape we should be, one minute thin is in, the next big is back. It's been the same throughout history, but then there's always been something to help you get into shape. Think yourself lucky you don't have to struggle into a set of these…

STAYS!

JUST WHEN YOU THOUGHT IT WAS SAFE TO GO BACK INTO THE WARDROBE – CERT 18

Have YOU got the "staying power" to sit through this gripping feature about corsets?

GASP! When you discover that the fiendish fashion contraptions known as corsets (or stays) have been around since at least the 16th century. They were invented to squash saggy bits of bodies into a fashionable shape. To do this all sorts of reinforcements were used, including wood, iron, steel, whalebone, walrus tusks and animal horns.

REEL! When you find out that in medieval times some corsets were made *entirely* from iron. One disadvantage of these sorts of corsets was that sweat from the wearer's body caused them to go rusty.

BLUSH! When you discover that corsets were also worn by men – particularly in early Victorian times – because they wanted everyone to think that they had figures like athletes.

GROAN! As you realize that between 1880 and 1905 corsets got tighter than ever. Women wore them so tightly that they fainted, their ribs broke and their internal organs were actually squeezed into the wrong places.

SIGH! When you learn that despite warnings from doctors about serious health risks, mums still insisted on squidging their daughters into corsets. In order to cram a poor girl in, she was made to lie face down on the floor and take a deep breath, they then placed one foot on her back and pulled the lace fasteners with all their might. This gripping exercise was said to turn a 15-year-old girl's 58 cm (23 inch) waist to a waist of only 33 cm (13 inches) in just two years.

SHUDDER! At a Victorian magazine article that described how the headmistress of a smart girls' boarding school personally sealed all the girls into their corsets. The prisoners (sorry ...) *pupils* had to keep them on at *all* times – apart from just one hour on Saturdays when they were allowed out for a wash!

AND THEN RELAX When you discover that corsets went out of fashion in the late 1950s – sensible people probably realized that the fashion had just been a *"waist of time"*! But it hasn't always been trendy to be as slim as a shoelace.

Absolutely flabulous fashion for men

At various times in the past extra bits of flesh have been considered beautiful – and additional bits like double chins, pot bellies and enormous bottoms have all had their moments. In the 15th and 16th centuries in Spain, if men couldn't achieve flab fast enough, they cheated!

No one is absolutely sure how the fashion for pease-cod bellies began but some fashion experts seem to think that it may have originally been worn as protective padding during sword fights (please treat this theory with caution – it may just be a gut feeling).

The most outstanding skirt of the 19th century

In the early 1850s a new shape hit the big time as it became fashionable for women to wear large bell-shaped skirts which made them look like enormous walking lampshades. At first, the only way women could create the crucial "rent-a-tent" dome-shape was to wear lots and lots of other skirts underneath them. These "under" skirts or "petticoats" were stiffened with horsehair – or *crin* as it was called by the French – which gave the style its name, "crinoline".

THE VIRTUOUS VICTORIAN JUST 1P

CRAZY CRINOLINES CAUSE CARRIAGEWAY CHAOS!

We are not amused! Have you seen them? These new-fangled crinolines? They're a crinoline waste of space if you ask us. Have women gone mad?

"Give us bigger crinolines!" we hear them cry.

"The bigger – the better! We want to knock people off the pavements, we want somewhere for small children and lost puppies to shelter during sudden showers of rain!"

And now … they're no longer satisfied with being moderately lampshade-shaped – they want to be the size of the dome on St Paul's Cathedral. So just to help them fulfil their fanatical fashion ambitions (and their skirts!) some nitwit has gone and invented a crinoline frame – a sort of a huge cage thingy so that these petticoat posers can make even *bigger* nuisances of themselves! It's a pity he didn't just make one great big crinoline cage – we could have locked up all the crazy crinolined women inside it and left them there until they came to their senses!

Five things we think our readers ought to know about these crinolines…

1 They prevent young men from kissing their sweethearts – we can't reach them!

2 They get jammed in doorways.

3 Two crinoline-wearing ladies can't even sit down on the same settee.

4 They're dangerous! If a lady in a crinoline stands too near an open fire, she goes up in smoke! We've even heard of one lady being blown into the sea and drowned!

5 And finally … errm … er … we've also been told that during extra long church services some ladies slip a chamber pot underneath their crinolines and have a crafty, err … tiddle!

CRINOLINE HALL
GREAT FROCKFORD
SKIRTFORDSHIRE

Dear Editor

I would like to respond to the article in yesterday's "Virtuous Victorian" by defending the crinoline.

1. Crinolines are fun. They show the confidence and optimism of our successful modern industrial age.

2. Crinoline's use masses of material – up to 44 metres (48 yards) – and provide jobs for thousands of textile workers.

3. Crinolines are comfortable – especially this new cage sort which keeps our petticoats away from our legs.

4. The crinoline is a real step forward for women and technology. The dress is made up on the wonderful new sewing machine that has freed so many women from hours of tedious hand-stitching.

5. Even the lowliest housemaid or factory girl can afford a crinoline. They provide a great opportunity for women from all walks of life to enjoy fashion for the very first time.

Yours expansively

Miss C. Shapechanger

Something to do
Make your own full-sized cage crinoline

What you need
- lots of "broadsheet" newspapers
- sticky tape
- eight metre-long strips of ribbon or tape
- an old belt or a piece of elastic (to fit around your waist)
- a stapler (preferably with staples in it)

What to do

1 Roll up one sheet of newspaper widthways as tightly as possible to make a long tube. Hold it together with a few strips of sticky tape.

2 Make a second tube. Make your two tubes into a circle like this...

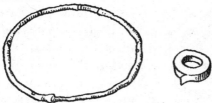

by squeezing the ends of one of the tubes and slotting them into the ends of the other, then taping the joins together with sticky tape.

113

3 Now make four more circles in the same way but each tube needs to be bigger than the last. Add an extra sheet of newspaper to each tube. You should end up with a total of five circles made with two, three, four, five and six tubes each.

4 Lay the circles on the floor with the smallest in the middle and the largest at the outside, like this:

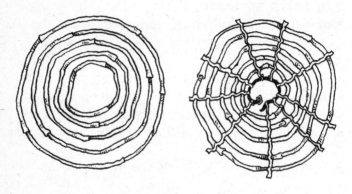

5 Lay the ribbon across the circles starting at the largest and finishing at the smallest – leaving about 12 cm (five inches) of the ribbon spare at the centre. Now carefully staple the ribbon to each hoop.

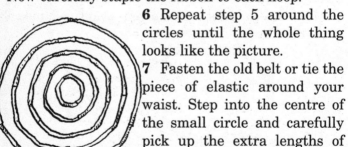

6 Repeat step 5 around the circles until the whole thing looks like the picture.

7 Fasten the old belt or tie the piece of elastic around your waist. Step into the centre of the small circle and carefully pick up the extra lengths of ribbon you left at the centre and tie them to the belt or elastic waistband.

Forever fab!

When the crinoline fashion finally fizzled out after 16 years or so women didn't just breathe a sigh of relief and say, "Thank goodness *that's* all over! At last, we can forget the whole thing and get back to being 'ordinary person' shaped!" Well, they wouldn't, would they? They were dedicated followers of smashin' fashion – they had to stay in style through thick and thin, *plus* lots of other shapes and sizes!

EXTRACTS FROM THE DIARY OF SMASHIN' FASHION FANATIC CELIA SHAPECHANGER

1870 Finally got rid of my crinoline - gave it to Hobbs (our manservant) He was really thrilled and says he can't wait to use it on family camping holidays! I'm not at all sorry to see it go (especially after the embarrassing church service incident!).

1871 Went shopping and bought a sort of strap-on pad contraption called a bustle (it's made from horsehair.) It's fantastic! Makes me look as if I've got a bottom the size of Birmingham! I also bought a new <u>extra tight</u> corset!

115

1875 Bustles are <u>OUT</u>. So I gave mine to Mrs Hobbs – she says it'll make a nice new hairpiece for Mr Hobbs. He's going a bit thin on top, apparently!

1882 Bustles are BACK! So I went shopping and bought the brilliant new CAGE sort. My bottom is now the size of a hot-air balloon!
My friend Amelia has got a folding one (bustle, that is – not bottom!) It's called the "langtry" and it sort of springs up when she sits down and snaps back into place when she stands up again.

1896 I've given my bustle cage to Hobbs... it's <u>so</u> old fashioned now (the bustle, not Hobbs – he lower class and has <u>never</u> been fashionable) He was very grateful and says it will come in handy for keeping his racing pigeons in!

1900 I went shopping and bought a new, longer corset, tighter than <u>ever</u>.
I gave my old one to Hobbs (not sure what he's intending to do with it) I am now a brilliant new super-fashionable "S" bend... which makes me stick out (rather a long way actually) at the back <u>and</u> the front!

1911 I went to a concert hall and saw a wonderful Russian ballet called "SCHEHEREZADE". The costumes were designed by an amazing chappie called BAKST. There were super bright colours, loose flowing shapes, silks, satins and velvets! Just heavenly! I must see my dress-maker immediately!

1912 I went shopping and bought a hat with a monster feather in it. It looks really spiffing with my new very tight "HOBBLE SKIRT" (totter, totter!) I look a bit like an 'oriental' character in that ballet I saw last year! So do all my friends!

1914 The war has started and I'm knitting socks for our troops. All the chaps are away fighting — women are doing the chaps' jobs!

1918 The war is over, hurrah! I must go shopping ... and see my dressmaker!

1920 I am now a new shape again! No sticky-out bits, and a short, straight haircut. I look a bit like a chap! Not sure I like it. Maybe I'm getting too old for this fashion lark!...

1924 I looked out of my bedroom window and I couldn't believe my eyes! I saw a young woman in the street ... WITHOUT A HAT! Didn't go shopping today. Couldn't face it.

1925 Bad day. I have taken to my bed after another terrible shock! My niece came to visit me in a SHORT SKIRT! It was KNEE LENGTH would you believe! I was able to see her (blush, blush) L·E·G·S! I feel faint ... I must find my smelling salts!

The end of the world is obviously due quite soon...

Short frock shock!

The First World War wasn't just about relations between countries. It caused a revolution in everyone's way of life. Women suddenly found they were needed in the workplace. In taking on the jobs that men had carried out before, they needed clothes that were practical to wear – and that meant sensible, comfortable shapes. Some women even took to wearing trousers – what was the world coming to? Fashion after the war would never be the same again, and practical shorter skirts were suddenly here to stay.

But 1925 was the first time that women had displayed their legs in public for hundreds of years. In Victorian times, just showing a bit of ankle was considered frightfully rude. So when the wild young fashion fanatics of the "roaring" 20s started showing as much as 25 cm (ten inches) of leg, older people were seriously shocked.

Smashin' fact

In 1925 the Bishop of Naples, in Italy, claimed that a recent earthquake had happened because God wanted to show everyone how annoyed He was about the new revealing fashion. And in America the state of Ohio introduced a law saying that any woman who wore her skirt higher than 7.5cm (three inches) above her ankle would be fined or imprisoned!

Rationed fashion

During the Second World War, in the 1940s, it was against the law to buy frivolous clothes. Materials were in short supply, so shorter skirts were helping the war effort! You were rationed as to how many clothes you could buy, so most people used to "make-do-and-mend". Magazine articles were full of wild ideas for brightening up old clothes.

Five steps to a wartime woman's wardrobe

1 Have a needle and thread at the ready, because patches are back! One magazine article says:

Patchwork ... is all you need to put life into our ration-weary wardrobe.

2 You'll have to make your own hats too – and you *will* be expected to wear one. In Paris, women are making hats from old curtains, plaited straw or coloured paper.

3 Embroidery, lace edging, turned-back cuffs and velvet collars are out – well, actually, they've been banned.

4 Bare legs are best. The government has banned silk stockings too – but American scientists are hurriedly experimenting with replacement fabrics. Nylon will follow shortly.

5 Stop showing off! Understatement is the order of the day. Keep your clothes simple, well-fitted and practical. As one magazine puts it, a well-dressed woman should, *"not be rendered helpless if stranded without a taxi."*

In 1947 a little-known designer called Christian Dior hit the big time with his "New Look" fashions. The war was over, rationing was on the way out, and make-do-and-mend had driven everyone round the bend. It was time for a change.

Smashin' fact

But some people were outraged by Dior's "New Look". Models parading the fashion on the Paris streets were attacked by protesters who tried to pull the dresses from their backs shouting, "40,000 francs for a dress and our children have no milk." The new fashions weren't available to everyone, but people with money were ready to spend it. By 1949 an evening dress from Dior might cost the same as a new car!

Another French designer whose clothes would probably have cost you a lifetime's pocket money was Coco Chanel. She's the subject of our next...

Smashin' fashion style profile

Gabrielle Chanel – French (1883–1971)

I thought you said her name was Coco?
No, Coco was her nickname, she was given it when she was a café singer during the 1900s.

Is it true she had a rough start in life?
Yes, she was abandoned by her dad when she was only 12 and had to go and live in an orphange.

So how did she get to be a smashin' fashion superstar?
While she was working as a dressmaker a few years later she met a fabulously wealthy man and went to live with him on his magnificent country estate. With a bit of help from his dosh and her own talent for design she was able to start her own fashion business. It was called Chanel Modes.

Hmm, very posh! She sounds like a stylish character?
She was. She became famous for something known as "classic chic".

What's that when it's at home?
It means using fashion simply but effectively

121

rather than going completely over the top.

So she wasn't into nine-inch platform soles and star-spangled cat suits?
She most certainly wasn't! She much preferred simple fashions like collarless cardigan suits worn with carefully chosen costume jewellery.

What was she most famous for?
During the early 1960s she came up with a little black dress that immediately became top of the frocks. It was known as...

Don't tell me, "the little black dress"?
You took the words right out of my wardrobe. Yes, every woman was supposed to have one of these dresses as a standby for those special occasions like cocktail parties, unexpected dinner invitations...

DINNER? TONIGHT? WHAT LUCK! I'M ALREADY DRESSED FOR IT!

And changing the baby's nappy?
Perhaps not.

Is it true she could be a bit bossy?
So they say. It's reported that once, when her workers were a bit miffed about their wages being cut, she got really angry and sacked the lot of them!

So they were run down by a cross Chanel fury!

You could say that!

You still hear her name quite a bit in the world of smashin' fashion.

Yes, you do, although she died in the 70s, her name lives on through things like the House of Chanel fashion business (now run by Karl Lagerfeld) and her famous and expensive *Chanel No. 5* perfume.

Not to mention her incredibly delicious Coco pops breakfast cereal!

Dimwit.

Smashin' fashion for revolting young people

All through the 20th century, fashion barriers have continually been broken down and older people have continually been shocked. You didn't have to be rich to be a fashionable 50s teenager, and you definitely didn't have to follow the style of your parents. Most teenagers prefered to look like a film star, and 50s stars didn't all go in for glamour. Parents thought their kids looked revolting wearing "work" clothes for best...

123

The black leather bomber jacket

German pilots in the First World War wore leather coats that had tails – they were a sort of fashion that was left over from the 19th century. When the pilots sat in the cramped cockpits of their aeroplanes the tails got in the way so they cut them off and ended up with a short leather jacket. This sort of jacket eventually became standard flying gear for fighter pilots in the Second World War and was named the "bomber" jacket. They became smashin' fashion wear in the 1950s when stars like Marlon Brando and James Dean wore them in films such as *The Wild One* (1953) and *Rebel Without a Cause* (1955).

Denim jeans

Up until the 1950s, jeans were just baggy unfashionable things that baggy unfashionable folk like farmers wore to work. Then, in the 1950s, an American actor called James Dean (him again) wore a pair in a film and everything changed. Suddenly jeans got trendy and they've stayed that way for more than 40 years. Sometimes they've been skin tight, sometimes they've been loose and sometimes they've been skin-tight and loose at the same time.

Smashin' facts

1 In the mid-19th century a man called Levi Strauss began selling tent and covered wagon canvas to gold miners in California. He made any spare canvas into trousers which he also

---

124

sold to the miners. They became known as Levis (not strousers?).

2 In 1860, casting aside the old tent fabric, Levi started using a new material that he dyed with a blue dye called indigo. The material came from Nimes in France and it was called "serge de Nimes" – or denim for short.

3 In 1870, Levi used metal rivets to re-inforce the seams. Now miners could stuff their pocket with gold – and there was no fear of losing it!

4 To prove how tough his denims were, Levi organized a publicity stunt. He got two horses to try to pull the jeans apart. They failed, the jeans survived, and Levi added a leather label on the back pocket that looks like this:

5 Since Levi made his first pair in 1850, over two billion pairs of jeans have been sold around the world.

And those jeans just wouldn't look the same without...

A vest

It's 1953 and young, smouldering, handsome heart-throb film hero Marlon Brando is appearing at a cinema near you, in a film called *The Wild Ones*. He is wearing a black leather bomber jacket, denim jeans and a vest as an overshirt – oo-er, it's supposed to be worn as underwear! He's about to change the face of fashion for ever.

Smashin' fact
T-shirts were first worn as underwear by American soldiers during the First World War. They came in handy in the Second World War, too, when the US Navy ordered thousands of new short-sleeved shirts for their sailors. They called the shirts T-types, because of their shape.

Seven and a half top ideas for trendy T-types

1 Go to work in it. OK, so it doesn't sound very exciting, but that's just what labourers used to use T-shirts for in the early part of the century – and they still do today!

2 Use it to advertise. T-shirts these days advertise just about anything. But the very first advertising T-shirt came out in 1939 to promote the film, *The Wizard of Oz*.

3 Stretch it into a T-shaped mini-dress. That's what Biba, the famous London fashion store, did in 1966, revealing a whole lot of leg – parents were shocked again. Less shockingly, in 1978 T-shirts stretched all the way back down to the ankles and became maxi-dresses.

4 Design-it-yourself. In the late 1960s, travellers to India and other faraway places came back with some groovy ethnic ideas and tie-dye T-shirts really took off. All you needed was an old vest, a few bits of string, and a packet of dye.

5 State your taste. Rock and pop T-shirts were top of the tops in the early 70s. Not only could you tell everyone who your favourite band was, but you could pay for the privilege, too!

At a weekend rock concert in 1978, heavy metal band, Led Zeppelin, sold 25,000 T-shirts.

6 Scratch and sniff it. A new range of T-shirts in the late 70s had smelly designs. They showed nice things like strawberries on the front and had a smell to match.

7 Make it talk. In 1984 Katherine Hamnett made a range of big baggy T-shirts with a message:

KATHERINE HAMNETT   NOT KATHERINE HAMNETT

7½ Rip it up! In 1976, if you were a punk, you could make a cheap fashion statement and outrage your elders at the same time by taking an old T-shirt (Noddy and Big Ears perhaps?), ripping it to shreds and wearing the half that was left with a few safety pins for decoration.

Now you can buy T-shirts with holograms, that glow in the dark, or change colour as the temperature changes. In the 80s you could even buy T-shirts with padded shoulders, thanks to the creative genius of our next fashion superstar...

Smashin' fashion style profile

Giorgio Armani – Italian (b.1935)

So what's all this about shoulders then?

Along with Versace, Giorgio is said to have started the craze for "power" suits for men and

128

THESE SHOULDER-PADS WILL TAKE ME RIGHT TO THE TOP - JUST AS SOON AS THEY WIDEN THE LIFT DOORS...

women back in the 1980s. Their characteristic was large padded shoulders and they were designed to help people get on in the world of business.

How did Giorgio shoulder his way into the world of fashion?

He started out as a window dresser. In 1975 he formed his own company and quickly became world famous for the clean, simple look of his clothes. He started the fashion for suits and dresses made from crumpled fabrics like linen.

I've heard that he can be a bit of a fuss pot?

Well, it's "alleged" that he's very particular about the way his business is run. For example, he's said to have specified the exact distance between each coat-hanger in every single one of his shops. He's got dozens and dozens of them all over the world, you know.

What coat-hangers?

No *shops*! ... He's got *millions* of coat-hangers!

His name seems to be everywhere.

That's because his fashion empire is absolutely enormous. He sells smashin' fashion to a vast range of customers and his business operates on different levels. You probably already know the names of his three most famous labels.

There's err ... "Emporio Armani?"
These are the less expensive designer label clothes.
And, "Collectione Armani?"
These are more expensive and exclusive clothes bought by people like politicians, footballers, TV celebrities...
Who like to spend a bit of dosh on cutting a bit of a dash?
Exactly!
In which case, what's the legendary Armani "Black Label" brand all about?
Oooh, those are the designer originals costing anything up to £2,000 which are bought by international superstars like Tina Turner, Harrison Ford, Steven Spielberg, Robert de Niro...
And by school teachers everywhere!
Of course!
Hmm ... Giorgious!

Something to do
Make a set of Giorgio Armani-style shoulder pads
What you need
- sticky tape
- two washing-up sponges
- scissors

What to do
1 Cut each washing-up sponge into a D-shaped pad.

2 Fold a length of sticky tape into a small loop with the sticky side facing outwards.

3 Stick it onto a pad – now repeat the process for the other one.

4 Attach the pads to the shoulders of your favourite sweater, jacket, dress (or T-shirt).

I'M REALLY SOAKING UP THE ATMOSPHERE!

5 Wear it when you launch your very own collection of fashion designs in the next chapter and be really ... *assertive!*

Handy tip Make sure you put the pads *inside* the shoulders of your garment otherwise you may quickly lose credibility with your designer chums.

IGNORE HIM – HE'S JUST A SPONGER!

And if you don't like the shape of things today, you can always have a go at changing them yourself! Take a few swift strides to the next chapter to find out how.

A FEW SWIFT STRIDES THROUGH THE HISTORY OF THE TROUSER

BRACCAE - FABRIC WRAPPED AROUND LEGS AND HIPS, OFTEN MADE FROM CHECKED MATERIAL. WORN BY EUROPEAN BARBARIAN TRIBES. INVADING ROMAN SOLDIERS THOUGHT THEY WERE VERY UN-TRENDY - BUT WORE THEM ANYWAY TO KEEP OUT THE NORTHERN CHILL.

BREECHES - KNEE LENGTH TROUSERS, GENERALLY WORN BY EUROPEAN MEN UNTIL THE 19TH CENTURY. UPPER CLASS BOYS IN THE 17TH CENTURY WERE "BREECHED" WHEN THEY WERE 8 YEARS OLD - UNTIL THIS AGE THEY WERE USUALLY "DRESSED" - IN DRESSES!

TRUNK HOSE - 16TH CENTURY - SHORT, PUFFED BREECHES, ATTACHED TO STOCKINGS OR TIGHTS BY LACES KNOWN AS "POINTS".

FARTHINGALE BREECHES WITH BUILT-IN PADDED HOOP IN FASHION FROM 1575 TO 1600 AD. KING CHARLES I OF ENGLAND WAS FOND OF THESE - THEY PROTECTED HIS TENDER BITS FROM SNEAKY SWORD THRUSTS...

FULL LENGTH BREECHES THIS EARLY VERSION OF MODERN TROUSERS WAS FIRST WORN BY FRENCH REVOLUTIONARIES IN THE 1790s, WHO WERE KNOWN AS THE "SANS CULOTTES" (BLOKES WITHOUT BREECHES). THEY ABANDONED KNEE BREECHES BECAUSE THAT FASHION WAS POPULAR WITH THE HATED ARISTOCRATS — AND STARTED A TREND WHICH HAS BEEN FOLLOWED EVER SINCE.

BELL BOTTOMS - BAGGY WITH FLARED BOTTOMS. WORN BY SAILORS SINCE THE 16TH CENTURY TO MAKE AWKWARD NAVAL MANOEUVRES EASIER - E.G RUNNING UP THE RIGGING, OR DANCING THE HORNPIPE.

BLOOMERS TURKISH-STYLE TROUSERS POPULARISED DURING THE 1850'S IN AMERICA BY WOMEN'S RIGHTS CAMPAIGNER AMELIA BLOOMER (1818-94) WORN UNDER KNEE-LENGTH SKIRTS AND SUITABLE FOR SPORTY ACTIVITIES LIKE TENNIS, CYCLING AND ARCHERY.

KNICKERBOCKERS KNEE-LENGTH TROUSERS WITH A BUCKLE AT THE KNEE. WORN FOR SPORT AND HOLS FROM THE 1860S ONWARDS, AND NAMED AFTER A CHARACTER IN A BOOK BY WASHINGTON IRVING. FASHIONABLE AGAIN WITH NEW ROMANTICS IN THE 1980S

PLUS FOURS
BAGGIER VERSION OF KNICKERBOCKERS. POPULAR IN THE 1920s AND '30s. FOUR INCHES OF EXTRA MATERIAL GAVE ADDED 'BAG'. HARDLY EVER SEEN NOWADAYS APART FROM FASHION MUSEUMS, GOLF COURSES... AND WEEKEND WEAR FOR TEACHERS...

OXFORD BAGS
ENORMOUS BAGGY TROUSERS WORN IN THE MID 1920s BY OXFORD UNIVERSITY STUDENTS. TROUSER HEMS WERE 50cm (16 ins) WIDE! CAME BACK FOR WOMEN IN THE 1930s AND 1960s

ZOOT TROUSERS
(BOTTOM HALF OF ZOOT SUIT) USUALLY IN BRIGHT COLOUR- REALLY BAGGY BUT VERY TIGHT AT ANKLE. WORN WITH MATCHING LONG JACKET, 1930s TO 1950s

PEDAL PUSHERS

TROUSERS FOR WOMEN -
WORN IN THE 1950s AND
REVIVED IN THE 1970s.
CALF LENGTH. GOOD
FOR CYCLING IN -
TROUSER CUFFS DON'T
GET CAUGHT IN THE
CHAIN !

DRAINPIPES

VERY TIGHT
TROUSERS WORN
BY 1950s
TEDDY BOYS...
(AND PLUMBERS?)

LOON PANTS 1970s

VERY FLARED TROUSERS -
TIGHT AT THE TOP AND
INCREDIBLY WIDE AT
THE BOTTOM. WEARERS
OFTEN DIDN'T SEE THEIR
FEET FOR WEEKS ON END!
MADE FROM SATIN, VELVET OR DENIM.
PATCHES, TASSELS AND BELLS SEWN ON.
WORN BY YOUNG PEOPLE, HIPPIES, ETC.

READY, STEADY, JET SET GO!

A smashin' fashion job

So you're crazy about clothes, fanatical about fashion and stuck on style! Fancy turning your passion for fashion into a successful career? Find out if you've got what it takes to make it in the global glamour industry by checking out the smashin' fashion...

Fashion model

You must be about 1.78 metres (6 feet) tall and "good looking" (whatever that means). You will work patiently for hours on end with photographers (who can sometimes be very difficult, darling). You will be told to turn this way and that, to smile, to snarl, to smoulder (and then burst into flames?). Your make-up will be constantly fiddled with and your hair will be continually messed with. At fashion shows you will be expected to change from one set of clothes to another in less time than it's taken you to read this sentence (all right so you're a slow reader!).

You must never have enormous pimples on the end of your nose (or anywhere else). You will be expected to rush off to exotic locations for fashion shoots at a moment's notice and then be paid vast amounts of money for spending hours sitting around doing absolutely nothing (as far as everyone else can see).

Warning! By the time you are 30 people will no longer telephone you with offers of work – as a model you will be past your bell by date! You will have no choice but to marry an ancient rock star.

Fashion photographer

You can be any height you like ... and look like the back end of a camel (optional) – but you will have to work patiently for hours on end with models (who can be very difficult, darling) using

your specialist skills, tonnes of high-tech camera equipment, flashy lighting aids and a few tricks of the trade involving things like pins and sellotape (to get rid of all those droopy, untidy bits!). Your mission (should you choose to accept it) will be to produce those almost too good to be true images of beautiful people that appear in fashion magazines and advertisements for trendy clothes, cars, holidays etc., etc.

Stylist

You will work with designers, models and photographers (who can all be very difficult, darling). Your task will be to ensure that the models always have an exciting and well co-ordinated overall "look". You must have a good sense of colour and design that will enable you to choose the sort of accessories and hairstyles that complement the features of the models and set off the designer's designs to perfection!

Fashion buyer

You will go to all the big fashion shows to look at the new season's styles, then buy lots of them for big department stores (but you won't be expected to carry them all back on your own!). You must have an instinctive feel for choosing the sort of 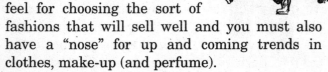 fashions that will sell well and you must also have a "nose" for up and coming trends in clothes, make-up (and perfume).

Important You must also have an "eye" for detail and be able to spot goods that are faulty or of poor quality.

Image consultant

You will be a bit like a stylist – but rather than working with the models you will advise other people involved in the fashion business on how they should look and behave so that they present a perfect image to everyone they meet (rather than just making them giggle with embarrassment).

You will give advice on important things that everyone who wants to be successful ought to know, such as what colours they should wear, what shapes of clothes suit their body best (how it's really uncool to walk round with your tongue hanging out ... or with your underpants on the top of your head, that sort of thing). You may wish to specialize in one aspect of image consultancy, such as, believe it or not ... smiling! Yes, ... "smile" consultants really do exist!

Public relations consultant

You will handle publicity and give out information on behalf of people working in the fashion business – where their next big shows are being held, what they think this season's big colour is going to be (where to get rid of last season's big colour?) etc.

Fashion journalist

You will write influential articles about fashion for newspapers and top fashion magazines like *Vogue, Harpers and Queen, Marie Claire* (and *Goat World*?). Your every word will be hung upon by fashion fanatics the world over – so if you say that peep-toe, lime green, Doc Martens with 25 cm (ten inch) stiletto heels are going to be this week's trend, people will be falling over themselves to keep up with this exciting new foot fashion!

Please apply for any of the above vacancies in writing (joined-up would be nice) enclosing a current photograph (preferably of you) – a full C.V. (not Citroen) – and stamped and really snazzily dressed envelope.

Important note If none of the above vacancies appeals to you, but you still want to work in the fashion world – you love combining colours, shapes

140

and textures in exciting ways – you are bursting with energy and creative ideas and desperate to get to the top – well, you could always become a fashion designer.

You've now reached the section where you can learn just that: how to become a top international fashion designer. And, to help you along the road to fame and fortune, we'll be stopping off at the Catwalk of Fame to pick up a few tips from a couple more of the super-designers who've made it really big (and small … and skimpy) in the world of smashin' fashion.

TEN STEPS TO BECOMING A TOP FASHION DESIGNER

Step one – get yourself a name

If you've got a name like Cynthia Shufflebottom or Darren Dudpud this could be a bit of a disadvantage in the image-conscious world of fashion. You're going to need a name with an international feel that immediately conjures up thoughts of exciting, glamorous, jetsetting life-styles – rather than boring Sunday afternoons spent helping Uncle Ron worm his whippets. Go for something like Venetia Vespucci, Paulo Pogo, Arny Baconburger or Tatiana

141

Tighttrousers. You'll be amazed at the difference a name makes!

Your new name is going to be *incredibly* important throughout your career – it's going to go on the label that will be attached to every single fashion item you sell, and don't forget, in the world of fashion an awful lot of people are obsessed with labels!

Important warning – up-and-coming fashion designers beware!

Someone who could probably sew his name into a pair of skunk's socks, and *still* sell them for a fortune is Calvin Klein. Calvin's international fashion business sells products ranging from perfume to underpants – and fashion fanciers everywhere pay oodles just so they can wear products bearing his distinctive CK logo. This is a pity really, because quite often these things aren't Calvin Klein originals at all … they're copies that have been "pirated" (passed off as originals) by

ruthless tricksters who are anxious to help themselves to a slice of Calvin's phenomenally profitable fashion action! So, be warned – watch out for people wearing designer eye patches and flared wooden legs – they're fashion pirates!

Smashin' fashion style profile

Calvin Klein – American (b.1942)

How did Calvin get his show on the road?
He began by studying the fashion business at the New York Fashion Institute of Technology.

It was obviously a perfect "F.I.T."! What sort of clothes is he best known for?
He designs clothes in natural fabrics like wool, silk and linen – his fashions are described as "understated". So rather than "shouting" at you they are more likely to "whisper".

Is it true that he had a bit of luck that gave him a big break?
Yes, it happened when an executive from a

famous American department store stepped out of a lift on the wrong floor and came face to face with a rack of CK fashion designs – he was knocked out by Calvin's clothes!

The next day Calvin wheeled the rack through the busy streets of New York so he could personally show them to the store's boss.

Couldn't he afford the bus fare then?

Of course he could! He transported them like that because he wanted the clothes to look absolutely perfect when they arrived. And it was all well worth it too – the store boss placed a huge order for his designs.

He sounds like he's a perfectionist?

He is! He can't stand to see wrinkles in material. He's so fussy about his own clothes that the moment he takes off his jacket, one of his staff of five helpers whips it straight onto an ironing board and irons it back to perfection.

So now you know – in addition to getting yourself a name that's constantly going to be on the tip of everyone's tongue as well as the tags on their T-shirts and trousers, you must also go to a lot of trouble with your personal appearance.

Step two – plan your collection

You must now begin to put a "collection" together – no, not stamps or fossils – but clothes! Yes, it's decision time – so ask yourself these questions!

a) What sort of clothes am I going to design – *who* are they going to be for ... boys, girls, men, women (hamsters)?

b) Where and when are my designs going to be worn – for leisure, for sport, for business (for a dare?) – during the day, in the evening (in the bath)?

c) Which of the two fashion seasons am I going to design my collection for – spring and summer or autumn and winter ... (or both)?

d) What colour theme should I choose for my collection? The fashion world usually decides about two years in advance what a particular season's colour is going to be so it's important to be in the know.

Step three – select your market

This means that you must decide on the sort of customers you're going to sell your smashin' fashions to. To find out a bit more about "who buys what", Chic Togs, the fashion and gossip correspondent, talked to some typical fashion fans...

Miss Ava Ridge (25) – school teacher

Miss A I buy my clothes from ordinary shops on the high street. I suppose designers would say that was "mass market". That means it's worn by ordinary people like mums, grans, dads … and teachers like me (we don't all go to charity shops, you know). And it's made out of material that doesn't cost loads, so the clothes are reasonably cheap.

The trouble with "mass market" clothes, though, is that anyone can buy them. That means it's not so easy to be different from the crowd. Last week I was at a party where a woman was wearing *exactly* the same dress as me. It didn't really matter. I just smiled and said, "Ha, ha – great minds think alike!" Then I locked her in a cupboard for the rest of the evening.

Arabella Absolutely-Rollinginit (24) – billionaire's daughter, charity skier

A.A-R. Mummy and daddy are absolutely stinking rich, so all the clothes I buy are *haute couture* fashions – that's French for "fine tailoring" you know. When I go out, I'm absolutely certain that no one else will be wearing the same dress as me, because there's only one dress

146

like it in the world – I've had it specially made for me, me, me.

Yes, it's bound to cost a lot more than your average grotty mass market grunge, but what's a few thousand pounds when you're rolling in lolly?

Apparently, there are only about 3,000 people like me in the whole wide world who can afford to buy *haute couture*. That does make me feel rather special.

Dave and Marcia – (26 and 27) – both work in the pop music industry

Marcia We're not as rich as Arabella, but we need to keep up with the trends in the music business. *Haute couture* is a bit out of our price range, but mass market stuff is a bit too ordinary. Instead we buy "designer label" fashions. They're somewhere between the two. They don't make too many of any one design, and they pay attention to details like  the quality of the material, the way a dress is cut, hand-stitching...

Dave Yeah, they tend to make sure you've got the right number of legs on your trousers and that the buttons stay on for at least two days.

Marcia Designer label clothes aren't as cheap as mass market stuff...

Dave So that's why we buy ours second-hand.

Tip Top designers aim for the posh end of the market because they know that cheaper and simplified versions of their styles will find their way into the "mass market" later on.

Step four – get inspired

Now you've got to think of a "theme" for your collection – for instance when Vivienne Westwood put on a show in 1983 she gave it a "witches" theme (and the whole thing was a wicked success!). So dream up your own theme by releasing your imagination into the community and allowing it to run riot – or at least become a bit playful. Let it scamper around for a bit and poke its nose into all of the exciting creative possibilities. Look for inspiration in things like:

Nature

Study the details of plants and flowers, animal patterns and colours, maybe even whole landscapes and skyscapes!

These are an inspiration to many designers – lots of fashions come around again and again, either in their original form or with a few changes. So why not have a swift "style-surf" through the centuries ... and then start some new crazes like: leather crinolines with optional studs and slashing ... tie-dyed peasecod body stockings ... winkle-picker trainers ... feathered baseball caps ... the possibilities are endless!

Art

IT'S INSPIRED BY THIS GREAT ABSTRACT PAINTING – AND IT DOESN'T MATTER IF YOU SPILL YOUR DINNER DOWN IT!

Look at the work of artists – notice the way they use colours, patterns and shapes – look at the subtle shades of the colours they use – think how you could combine them for maximum effect.

Smashin' fashion style profile

Jean-Paul Gaultier – French (b.1952)

Jean-Paul Gaultier is a fashion designer whose work, he says, is inspired by artists – especially the vibrant colours and the bold shapes of the French painter Henri Matisse (1869–1954). He's on the Smashin' Fashion Catwalk of Fame right now with gossip correspondent Chic Togs. Jean-Paul is looking sensational wearing his own fabulous designs...

C.T. Bonjour Jean-Paul!
J-P Bonjour, Chic ... bonjour, fashion furns.
C.T. So Jean-Paul, tell us 'ow, sorry ... how you got started?
J-P Ah didn't 'ave ze college training in ze fashion business. When ah wurz a teenager ah began sketching designs for collections of clothes. Ah sent ma sketches to ze top designers. Ze famous French fashion designer Pierre Cardin...
C.T. ... Cardigan?
J-P Non, Cardin! ... 'e saw zem and invatted me to work for 'im for a year. Ah learned everysing about ze fashion creation wiz 'im ... le designing, le pattern cutting, le sewing and fitting ze

clothes … ze lot! Ah also learned a lot from studying fashion magazines.

C.T. You must have been bursting with confidence!

J-P Yes, ah wurz. Ah set up ma own business in 1977. Ah 'ave been creating ever since. Look 'ere is a supermodel wearing some of ma most famurz togs.

C.T. Oh, they're fabulous … and so "witty"!

J-G Ha … ha! Zat is right, Chic! Ah like to make ze jokes with ma clothes – jurst take un butcher's at zis rough, tough, sporty sweatshirt zat Mungo is wearin' – ah 'ave trimmed it wiz ze lace and satin – it eez a rat giggle … eez it nurt?

C.T. Hmmm … smashin'!

Feeling inspired by art, nature, or wacky Jean-Paul? Bursting with ideas? Good! Take out those felt-tip pens and coloured pencils and … get designing!

Step five – make your design

Most fashion designers start with a drawing – this is what is known as a *two-dimensional* design – it will later become a *three-dimensional* design in the shape of some finished fashion wear (hopefully!).

151

Four trendy tips

1 Your creations must have "hanger appeal" – this is the fashion designer's way of saying that they will look almost as good hanging from rails in shops as they do when they're draped on your magnificent models. If you're going to succeed, your styles have got to stand out from everyone else's designs and grab the attention of fashion addicts.

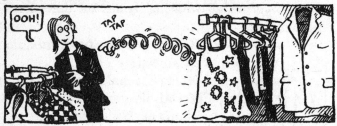

2 If you don't want to start from scratch with your collection, why not recycle other people's cast-offs? You can modify old clothes by doing things like: adding some sequins to an old pair of gloves, spraying your mum's old wellies silver and sticking some plastic flowers on them; turning an old dress into some stunning beach- or disco-wear – but don't forget to ask first!

This sort of DIY "street fashion" has inspired the likes of Vivienne Westwood and Zandra Rhodes.

3 As well as recycling unwanted clothes why not do your bit for the environment and turn a few other discarded items into smashin' fashion?

In February 1996, a "Recycled Fashion Show" was held at the Kensington and Chelsea Town Hall in London. The highlights of the show included:

- a cocktail dress made from soft drinks cans
- jewellery made from ring pulls

- a full length gown made from old rubber washing-up gloves and scouring pads and...
- a handbag made from a wellington boot!

So get cracking – turn those old crisp packets and unwanted washing-up liquid bottles into some snappy designer disco clobber!

4 As the ideas come thick and fast and you start to design the styles that will be on everyone's backs, bottoms and bedroom floors for months to come remember to keep your creations under your hat (or your bed).

Smashin' facts

1 When British royals Charles and Di got married in 1981, Di wanted a wedding dress that was absolutely unique. She asked David and Elizabeth Emmanuel to design it for her. Every detail had to be kept absolutely top secret. When the big day came, and Di appeared in the dress at last, mass-market designers had their pencils poised ready to make sketches of the dress and rush their designs to clothes manufacturers who were all set to work through the night. Cheaper copies of Di's dress were available in the shops the very next day!

2 In 1977 Elsa Schiaparelli had one of her dress

designs transported to a fashion show at the Ritz Hotel in an armoured car – well, it was priced at £1,000,000 (one million pounds) and decorated with 516 diamonds (the dress, not the car!).

Tip Save yourself the trouble of hiring a fleet of armoured cars for your creations – just keep them in polythene bags (bin liners are ideal).

Step six – decide where you're going to launch your collection

The big fashion shows are held in places like New York, London, Paris, Milan and Tokyo – if you've got a pocket money problem, or some rather pressing homework commitments that prevent you from getting to these international venues, why not hold the show in your front room, garden or school hall?

Step seven – sign up some models

You will need a few supermodels to wear your designs at the launch. There's no point in approaching a top star like Naomi Campbell because she says that she, "won't get out of bed for less than £10,000" (her trips to the bathroom must cost a fortune!). So it might be a better idea to use a few pals to show off your clothes – but remember, your models can make or break your big day – so give them a few tips about modelling first!

Dear Model
Re: The Zabaglione "launch"
Here are a few tips to help you through our big day:

A) Look cheerful... or snooty... but never gormless.

B) Walk quickly, confidently and importantly – but not so quickly that you fall off the end of the catwalk.

C) Let your warm and attractive personality radiate out to the audience – but NO blowing them kisses, singing chart hits or telling corny jokes.

D) Perform all-important super model twirl and turn perfectly so that you show my designs off to their best advantage – but don't twirl too vigorously or your flying skirt may knock the wig off the incredibly important top fashion journalist who is going to be sitting in the front row.

It is also ESSENTIAL that you learn to change from one outfit into another in the blink of a false eyelash – and (despite the excitement of the occasion) remain <u>cool</u> and <u>calm</u> at all times.

Please avoid doing SILLY THINGS - like rushing out onto the catwalk with your shoes on the wrong feet, both legs in one trouser-hole, hangers still inside your dress. etc.

Best of luck — Z xxx

Step eight – send out invitations

> Dear important and influential
> Fashion World person —
> # EMPORIO ZABAGLIONE
> ("The cradle of cool")
> ...would like to invite you to the launch
> of the 'Cred Thred' Collection. So please
> come along to: the Front Room, My House,
> Style Street, Trendytown
> on Funday 1st of Marry
> Nibbles provided
> P.S – Don't forget your chequebook.

The idea is to get people who will help your career to attend the show, so get started on that list.

Definitely invite:

a) Top fashion journalists – who will be so stunned by your collection that they will all give it marks of 100 out of ten in the newspapers the very next day.

b) Photographers – who will take photographs that make your smashin' fashion designs look so good that you don't even recognize them yourself.

156

c) Buyers from the best and biggest stores all over the world – who will peer at your designs very, very carefully through their very, very dark glasses and then (with a bit of luck) order juggernaut loads of them.

d) Showbiz celebrities and rich people in general, who will be so mesmerized by your exclusive "originals", that they will hand over huge amounts of money for them.

Do **not** invite:

a) Rival fashion designers who will make rapid sketches and take sneaky snaps of your brilliant ideas throughout the show then rush back to their studios, add a few ideas of their own, knock up copies of your "exclusives" and have them in the shops (at loads cheaper prices!) before you've even finished sweeping up after your show.

b) Uncle Ron.

c) His whippets.

I NEVER GET INVITED TO ANY TOP FASHION SHOWS...

Step nine – crank up some razzmatazz!

You must create the right sort of atmosphere for your launch – fashion shows are like theatrical performances and must excite the imaginations of the audience. Jean-Paul Gaultier sometimes accompanies his shows with unusual sound effects, like Buddhist prayers and the sound of chanting monks.

Create exciting lighting effects – maybe with a battery of strobes, neons and holograms? If you don't happen to have any of these handy why not just try flicking the light on and off as your models parade up and down (then again perhaps not you might end up fusing the whole lighting circuit!). Also, as your models strut stylishly along the catwalk play some pop music to get the audience in a happy (and money-spending) frame of mind – make sure it's not *too* exciting though, you don't want them leaping out of their seats and boogying in the aisles – remember it's a fashion show, not an end of term disco!

Step ten – be a phenomenal success

That's it then … you've done it! You've successfully launched your first ever smashin' fashion collection. No doubt you're still reeling from the rapturous applause of the audience and more to the point you can't believe the vast order you've just been given by the buyer from that chain of internationally famous fashion stores – you know, the one who's just said she'll take 1,000 of your wackily original PVC sack dresses (or "bin liners" as other people prefer to call them!).

EPILOGUE

If one did not dress like other people, one should be pointed at as one went along!

That's what one aristocratic Englishwoman told the *London Magazine* in 1768. But walking around with a huge haystack on your head seems an awfully strange way of *not* drawing attention to yourself.

Fashion is even bigger business now than it was back in the 18th century, and people will put up with all sorts of discomforts to wear something because they think they ought to keep up with the trends. That can take up a terrific amount of time, money and energy. But as one wise fashion critic said, "You don't have to be fashionable to be stylish."

The clothes you wear say something about the kind of person you are, whether they're actually fashionable or not. And you can have a lot of fun with fashion just deciding what suits *you*, and which styles *you* like best.

So, be adventurous. Wear whatever smashin' fashions you like – and most importantly, have a smashin' time doing it!